EYEW   L

W9-BMN-743

TOP 10
CRETE

ROBIN GAULDIE

Penguin
Random
House

Top 10 Crete Highlights

The Top 10 of Everything

CONTENTS

Crete
Area by Area

Streetsmart

The information in this DK Eyewitness Top 10 Travel Guide is checked regularly. Every effort has been made to ensure that this book is as up-to-date as possible at the time of going to press. Some details, however, such as telephone numbers, opening hours, prices, gallery hanging arrangements and travel information are liable to change. The publishers cannot accept responsibility for any consequences arising from the use of this book, nor for any material on third party websites, and cannot guarantee that any website address in this book will be a suitable source of travel information. We value the views and suggestions of our readers very highly. Please write to: Publisher, DK Eyewitness Travel Guides, Dorling Kindersley, 80 Strand, London WC2R 0RL, Great Britain, or email travelguides@dk.com

Within each Top 10 list in this book, no hierarchy of quality or popularity is implied. All 10 are, in the editor's opinion, of roughly equal merit.

Front cover and spine *Balos Bay and Gramvousa, Chania*
Back cover *Agios Nikolaos at sunrise*
Title page *Venetian fortress Frangokastello, Chania*

Welcome to
Crete

Snowcapped mountains. Sandy beaches backed by palms. Turquoise-blue lagoons. Home of the ancient Minoans, a creative people who built their palaces here some 4,000 years ago. This is Crete, an extraordinary island that rises from the Mediterranean Sea south of mainland Greece. With Eyewitness Top 10 Crete, it's yours to explore.

The Minoans, who never developed an army since they had no enemies, are considered the world's first leisure civilization. So it seems appropriate that today, each summer, tens of thousands of holiday-makers flock to their island to bask in blissful sunshine and carefree escapism. Nowadays, visitors are attracted by Crete's golden sands and glistening waters, the informal seafood tavernas and hospitable locals, and the magnificent Venetian-era port cities of Irakleio, Chania and Rethymno.

Others come here to trace Crete's history and culture – to explore the timeless archaeological sites of **Ancient Knossos**, **Gortys**, **Phaistos** and **Gournia**, and to visit the fascinating **Irakleio Archaeological Museum** and the melancholic **Moni Arkadiou**. Adventurous outdoor enthusiasts are drawn to Crete's wild and dramatic unspoiled interior. They visit to hike the length of the **Samaria Gorge** or to cycle through the **Amari Valley** at the foot of **Mount Idi**. The foodies among them stop off at farm-shops, wineries and traditional tavernas to taste and buy wholesome local produce.

Whether you're staying for a weekend or a week, our Top 10 guide brings together the best of everything that Crete can offer, from Ancient Knossos to the romantic harbour town of Chania. The guide gives you tips throughout – from seeking out what's free to avoiding the crowds – plus five easy-to-follow itineraries, designed to help you visit a clutch of sights in a short space of time. Add inspiring photography and detailed maps, and you have the essential pocket-sized travel companion. **Enjoy the book, and enjoy Crete.**

Clockwise from top: **View of Loutro; windmills on the Lasithi Plateau; Moni Arkadiou; the fortress of Frangokastello; murals at Knossos; the harbour at Chania; the lagoon at Balos**

Exploring Crete

Crete is vast, stretching 260 km (162 miles) from east to west, and it really warrants at least one week, ideally two. Here are ideas for fitting the highlights – including ancient and modern sites, and indoor and outdoor activities – into a tight schedule. You'll need a car to keep up with these densely packed itineraries.

This fresco fragment is from Ancient Knossos.

The Venetian fortress at Rethymno sits on a rocky spur overlooking the sea.

Key
— Two-day itinerary
— Seven-day itinerary

Two Days in Crete

Day ❶
MORNING
Start at **Ancient Knossos** (see pp12–13), the ruins of a Minoan palace. Next, head to **Irakleio** (see pp16–17), Crete's capital, and explore the collection at the **Irakleio Archaeological Museum** (see pp18–19).
AFTERNOON
Spend the afternoon in Irakleio, with its car-free old town full of Venetian-era monuments. Later, drive to **Chania** (see pp20–21) and dine on local seafood. Spend the night there.

Day ❷
MORNING
Wander around Chania, with its pretty fishing harbour and colourful market. Drive to **Rethymno** (see pp26–27) and arrive in time for lunch.
AFTERNOON
Explore Rethymno's Venetian fortress, then take time for a swim at the palm-lined beach east of the harbour. Return to Irakleio in the evening for dinner.

Seven Days in Crete

Day ❶
Devote your first day to **Chania** (see pp20–21), with its lovely old town. Visit the **Archaeological Museum** (see p49), then enjoy a swim at **Oasis Beach** (see p21). Have dinner at **Portes** (see p109) and drinks at **Synagogi Bar** (see p108).

Day ❷
Devote today to a full-day excursion to the **Samaria Gorge** (see pp30–31). Wear good walking boots and carry a picnic lunch and plenty of water. This dramatic hike brings you down to the south coast at **Agia Roumeli** (see p65), with its black-sand beach. Have a swim, then take the coastal ferry to Chora Sfakion, where a bus will take you back to Chania.

The beach at Matala, on Crete's southern coast, is sheltered by red cliffs.

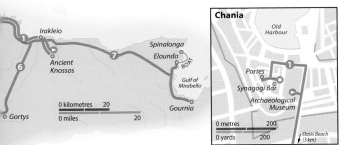

Day ❸

Drive along the coast to **Rethymno** *(see pp26–7)* and explore the old town's Venetian monuments. After lunch, go for a swim at Rethymno's palm-lined beach. Dine at **Avli** *(see p109)*, then go for cocktails at the **Garden of Ali Vafi** *(see p108)*.

Day ❹

Explore Western Crete's interior. Drive to the fortified monastery of **Moni Arkadiou** *(see pp36–7)*, with its 16th-century church and museum. Proceed to the remote **Amari Valley** *(see pp32–3)*, dotted with rural villages and Byzantine churches. Return to Rethymno for dinner.

Day ❺

Drive westwards to **Ancient Knossos** *(see pp12–13)* to see the ruins of this splendid Minoan palace. Later, head to **Irakleio** *(see pp16–17)*, where you can explore the wonderful Venetian old town and see the impressive treasures at the **Irakleio Archaeological Museum** *(see pp18–19)*.

Day ❻

Drive south across the island to two more archaeological sites: Roman **Gortys** *(see pp28–9)* and Minoan **Phaistos** *(see pp24–5)*. Take some time to explore the caves and relax on the white sand at **Matala** beach *(see p93)* before returning to Irakleio.

Day ❼

On your final day, head east along the coast to **Gournia** *(see pp34–5)*, another impressive Minoan site. Afterwards, have lunch in **Elounda** *(see p110)*. Take an afternoon boat trip from Elounda to the island fortress of **Spinalonga** *(see p111)*, rising from the clear blue waters of the Gulf of Mirabello. Return to Irakleio for the evening.

Top 10 Crete Highlights

The mosque within the ruined
Venetian fortress of Rethymno

🔟 Crete Highlights

Although it belongs to Greece, Crete has its own clearly defined history and folklore. The Minoans flourished here over 4,000 years ago. Greeks, Romans, Byzantines, Saracens, Venetians and Ottomans also left their mark. This rich heritage is set against magnificent mountain scenery and beaches lapped by a deep-blue sea.

Ancient Knossos ①
An impressive relic of the ancient Mediterranean world, the Minoan palace was imaginatively reconstructed in the early 1900s *(see pp12–15)*.

② Irakleio
A good place to see a slice of everyday Greek life, Crete's capital is an eclectic mix of medieval Venetian fortifications, bustling markets and modern streets *(see pp16–19)*.

③ Chania
Once the island's capital, this pretty little harbour town, with good beaches nearby and plenty of open-air restaurants and shops, makes a great base for exploring Crete's wild west *(see pp20–21)*.

④ Phaistos
One of the main Minoan sites in Crete, Phaistos is a maze of courtyards and stairways on a hillside overlooking the Messara Plain and the Libyan Sea *(see pp24–5)*.

Rethymno 5

Crete's third-largest city has had a multilayered history. A huge castle, Ottoman mosques, Venetian town houses and busy markets are part of the charm, along with a beach esplanade *(see pp26–7)*.

6 Gortys

Toppled Roman columns, the ruins of a Byzantine basilica, post-Minoan fortifications and remains of temples all hint at Gortys's chequered past *(see pp28–9)*.

Samaria Gorge 7

The "White Mountains" of the Sfakia region dominate southwest Crete. This rugged massif, most of which can be explored only on foot, is traversed by the lovely Samaria Gorge *(see pp30–31)*.

Sea of Crete

Irakleio · Limin Chersonisos · Aghios Ióannis · Sideros · Malia · Neapolis · Anogeia · Ancient Knosos · Oros Dikti · Agios Nikolaos · Siteia · Val · Kato Zakros · Oros · Panagia · Agioi Deka · Marta · Gournia · Sikea · Makrygialos · Gortys · Pirgos · Ierapetra

8 The Amari Valley and Mount Idi

Old-fashioned villages and legend-laden caves can be explored with a car or on a guided coach tour *(see pp32–3)*.

9 Gournia

Crete's best-preserved Minoan town has a labyrinth of tiny houses and narrow lanes surrounding a small palace overlooking the Gulf of Mirabello *(see pp34–5)*.

Moni Arkadiou 10

A place of tranquillity with a tragic past, the 16th-century Moni Arkadiou is Crete's best-loved Greek Orthodox monastery *(see pp36–7)*.

★ Ancient Knossos

Knossos is steeped in mystery and enchantment. In legend, it was the seat of King Minos, beneath whose palace the bull-headed Minotaur hunted its victims in the labyrinth built by Daedalus. In reality, it was the hub of a Bronze Age empire that held sway over the Aegean more than 4,000 years ago. This part of the Knossos story began to be unearthed during the early 1900s, when British archaeologist Sir Arthur Evans began excavations of the site.

1 Piano Nobile
Dubbed the "noble hall" because it might have been the audience hall of the Minoan kings, this vast room features copies of the fabulous frescoes of leaping bull dancers – Knossos's most famous images.

2 Storehouses
The storehouses contain giant earthenware jars **(above)**, which the Minoans used to keep olive oil, olives, grain and other supplies. Such jars (*pithoi* in Greek), with a capacity of up to 200 litres, are still made today.

3 Central Court
All Minoan palaces were built around a central courtyard. This would have been the hub of the complex and likely been used for ceremonial purposes and for royal audiences. The courtyard of Knossos has a view of the valley.

4 Throne Room
Here, a stone throne stands next to a basin believed to have been used for ritual purification, perhaps before sacrifices were made to honour the gods.

5 Dolphin Frescoes
The queen's rooms were decorated with frescoes of leaping dolphins **(below)**, and equipped with a bath and even a flush lavatory.

Plan of Knossos

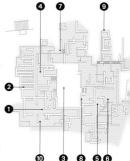

6 Hall of Double Axes

The hallway leading to the King's chamber is named after the double-bladed axe symbols carved into its walls and columns.

7 North Entrance Passage

A fresco of a bull adorns the entrance to this passage **(below)**. Images of sacred bulls outlasted the Minoan civilization and helped foster the legend of the Minotaur.

8 Great Staircase

Three smaller stairways and a maze of corridors would once have led off the five broad, shallow stone steps of the grand staircase **(below)**. Four of these wide steps survive to this day.

9 Bust of Sir Arthur Evans

A bust of Evans at the site entrance honours the man who first traced the palace of King Minos to this hillside above Irakleio. His sweeping reconstructions of the ancient palace owe much to his imagination.

10 South Portico

The south gateway to the palace complex **(left)** features copies of the Procession fresco, the original of which is in the Irakleio Archaeological Museum *(see pp18–19)*.

NEED TO KNOW

MAP K4 ▪ Route 97, 8 km (5 miles) S of Irakleio ▪ 2810 231940

Open summer: 8am–8pm daily (last entry 7:45pm); winter: 8am–3pm daily; closed or short hours on some national hols

Adm €15; concessions €8; combined ticket for Knossos and Irakleio Archaeological Museum *(see pp18–19)* €16

Disabled access difficult

▪ If possible, visit Knossos in spring or autumn, when cooler weather makes exploring more pleasant than in high summer.

However, if you are visiting in peak season, get to the site as soon as it opens, before most coach tour groups have arrived.

▪ There are several popular tavernas and decent snack bars within a few steps of the site entrance, along the main road to Irakleio.

Archaeologists in Crete

The Irakleio Archaeological Museum, established by Joseph Hatzidakis

1 Joseph Hatzidakis

Crete's own Joseph Hatzidakis pioneered the search for relics of the island's distant past, winning permission from the Ottoman sultan to establish the Cretan Archaeological Society in the 1880s. The Society played a key role in locating and preserving Crete's major sites, and in setting up the Irakleio Archaeological Museum *(see pp18–19)*.

Portrait of Heinrich Schliemann

2 Heinrich Schliemann

A famous archaeologist fascinated with the world of Homer's epics, Schliemann discovered first the site of ancient Troy (in Turkey), then Mycenae (in mainland Greece). In 1887, he turned his attention to sites in Crete, but he was unable to purchase the site of Knossos, leaving the field open for Sir Arthur Evans.

3 Sir Arthur Evans

Born into a wealthy British family, Sir Arthur Evans was educated at Oxford, where he later became keeper of the prestigious Ashmolean Museum. Crete's liberation from Ottoman rule in 1898, four years after his first visit to the site, made it possible for him to buy the site and begin work there in 1900. He devoted the next three decades of his life to Knossos.

4 Federico Halbherr

An Italian, Halbherr came to Crete in 1884 and befriended the Cretan archaeologist Joseph Hatzidakis, with whom he discovered the Bronze Age relics at the Dikteon Cave *(see p112)*. He later unearthed the palace sites at Phaistos *(see pp24–5)* and Agia Triada *(see p90)*.

5 John Pendlebury

One of the most colourful figures in Cretan archaeology, Pendlebury continued Evans' work at Knossos. He explored much of the island on foot and by donkey, pinpointing dozens of important sites. He also became a hero to Cretans after dying in action against the invading Germans in 1941.

6 Harriet Boyd-Hawes

This American archaeologist and nurse arrived on the island of Crete in 1900 and, after hunting for promising sites, surprised the archaeological world by unearthing a complete Minoan town at Gournia between 1901–1904 (see pp34–5).

7 Richard Seager

Among the first American scholars to work in Crete, Richard Seager excavated the Minoan site at Vasiliki at the beginning of the 20th century, before starting work at Mochlos (see p114), where American archaeologists still work with Greek researchers today.

8 Alan Wace

The prominent director of the British School at Athens, Alan Wace clashed with the opinionated Arthur Evans when his discoveries at Mycenae on the mainland led him to claim (correctly) that the Mycenaean culture had not been an offshoot of the Minoan, but had existed independently and had eventually come to control Knossos.

9 Minos Kalokairinos

This Cretan businessman and amateur archaeologist first dug at Knossos in 1878, finding fragments of Mycenaean pottery and large storage jars, but was unable to buy the site. His discoveries brought Knossos to the attention of Heinrich Schliemann.

10 Nikolaos Platon

The instincts of this Greek archaeologist led to the rediscovery in 1961–2 of the overlooked palace site at Zakros (see p42). The main clue to its existence was the natural harbour, as Platon suspected the site had once been an important trading city.

Zakros, rediscovered by Platon

THE DISCOVERY OF KNOSSOS

Sir Arthur Evans was inspired to dig at Knossos by the great German archaeologist Heinrich Schliemann, whose inability to purchase the site prevented him from excavating what he was convinced was a major Minoan palace. Evans, who excavated the long-lost Minoan palace at Knossos between 1900 and 1931, stands accused by some archaeologists of an excessively speculative reconstruction of the site, especially the upper floor which he dubbed the "Piano Nobile". Evans was attempting to bring to life an initially obscure and mysterious site, and his guesswork is perhaps excusable. Less admirable is the arbitrary placing of the brightly coloured "Minoan" frescoes, which are in fact 20th-century re-creations by Piet de Jong and Emile Gilliéron, some of them based on mere fragments of the original paintings.

Colourful fresco of water carriers

Irakleio

A massive medieval fortress still guards the harbour where the galleys of the Serene Republic of Venice once moored. Centuries-old churches and ornate fountains are other reminders of Irakleio's Venetian era. Busy open-air markets and the island's most fascinating museum are also attractions. Find a café table on one of the central squares and watch the busy everyday life of a Greek city, or browse the markets for Cretan handicrafts and delicacies to take home.

1 Morosini Fountain

Carved stone lions, the symbol of St Mark, decorate a small fountain **(below)** in the hub of Irakleio's old quarter. It is named after a late 17th-century doge of Venice.

Irakleio

2 Venetian Fortress (Koules)

The massive walls of the square fortress **(below)** were strengthened by the Venetians as the Ottoman threat grew during the 16th century.

3 Irakleio Archaeological Museum

This archaeological museum has an unrivalled collection from ancient Minoan, Greek and Roman cities *(see pp18–19)*.

4 Natural History Museum

This museum offers an impression of the Cretan landscape in Minoan times, before the importation of tamarisks, eucalyptus and bougainvillea. There are also stuffed animals, fossils and crystals.

7 Venetian Arsenals

The great wooden war galleys that gave Venice its maritime supremacy were built and repaired in vaulted arcades on the harbourfront opposite the fortress. Wooden fishing boats are still hauled up here for regular maintenance.

5 Venetian Bastions

Irakleio's Venetian walls **(above)** are surprisingly intact, though among a tide of modern buildings. Admire them from outside the Chania Gate, with its elaborate carving. Next to it is the massive Pantokratoros Bastion.

8 Agios Titos

A church dedicated to St Titus, the first bishop of Crete, has been on this site since the 10th century. The present structure **(below)** dates from the 1800s. Both church and saint are cherished by locals, as Titus is the patron of Crete.

IRAKLEIO'S STORY

The Andalucian Arabs who occupied Crete between 824 and 961 built a stronghold on the site of an earlier Roman settlement named Heracleum after the Greek hero Herakles (Hercules). Byzantine ruler Nikephoros Phokas renamed it Handax, which became Venetian Candia, then Ottoman Kandiye, while Cretan Orthodox dubbed it Megalo Kastro. Irákleio, so re-named from 1913, was heavily bombed during World War II, but became Crete's capital in 1971.

9 Market

The old market has striped awnings and counters piled high with everything from live snails to myriad varieties of Greek olives.

10 Historical Museum of Crete

This museum's proudest possessions are the only two paintings by El Greco to have been retained in the artist's native Crete. There are also some lovely stone pieces and traditional costumes *(see p90)*.

6 Museum of Religious Art

The world's finest collection of Cretan icons can be seen in this pretty 15th-century church. Glowing depictions of saints and martyrs, some in elaborate frames, adorn the walls. Three works by Michael Damaskinos: the *Adoration of the Magi*, *Last Supper*, and *Christ Appearing to the Holy Women*, are here.

NEED TO KNOW

Map K3

Greek Tourism Office: 1 Xanthoudidou; 2810 228225; open May–Sep Mon–Fri 9am-5pm; closes 3pm otherwise

■ To see the market at its best, arrive early, when the stalls are still piled high. The market remains open all day, Monday to Saturday, but most produce traders have packed up by midday.

■ Plateia Venizelou (Lion Square) is an ideal spot for a drink and a rest after a morning exploring the market and city.

Irakleio Archaeological Museum

An ornate item of Minoan jewellery

1 Minoan Jewellery and Helmets

Gold necklaces, pendants, rings, seals, sword hilts and helmets are among the many finds from Knossos, Phaistos and Gortys. Known for their love of beauty and refinement, the Minoans produced intricately crafted jewellery, decorated with flowers and animals, and sometimes set with semi-precious coloured stones.

2 Hall of Frescoes

Upstairs, the museum displays lively and colourful, but heavily retouched, Minoan frescoes from Knossos, Agia Triada and other palaces. Although notionally ancient, most of what is visible is early 20th century brushwork. Some of the most extraordinary depict bull-leaping performed by young acrobats, both male and female, who would run, grab the bull by its horns and somersault over its back. Archaeologists are still undecided as to whether this was a sport or a religious ritual.

3 Miniature Figures

Doll-like figurines of people and animals look like toys but are believed to have had a religious purpose as votive offerings. Most were found in mountain sanctuaries and caves, such as the Dikteon (Psychro) Cave *(see p112)*. The figures offer an important insight into contemporary fashions, along with an indication of gestures of worship.

Display of miniature figures

4 Agia Triada Sarcophagus

This elaborately painted stone coffin is adorned with depictions of animal sacrifices, a funeral

Beautiful example of the frescoes decorating the palace at Knossos

The Agia Triada Sarcophagus

Phaistos Disc

8 This 4,000-year-old clay disc is embossed with symbols believed to be the earliest example of a form of printing. The hieroglyphics on the disc, which was unearthed at Phaistos in 1903, are the earliest-known Minoan script. No one has yet succeeded in deciphering the full text, so its meaning remains a mystery, though some archaeologists claim to have decoded the words "goddess" and "mother".

procession, women riding chariots pulled by slaves, and mythical beasts. It was perhaps made for a Minoan ruler.

Bull's Head Rhyton

5 Fashioned in the shape of a bull's head, this 16th-century BC wine vessel is carved from black steatite stone and has a mother-of-pearl snout, gilded horns, and rock crystal eyes. It was discovered at Knossos and probably used in ritual.

Rhyton shaped like a bull's head

Town Mosaic

9 Glazed tiles, each depicting multi-storey buildings of the Minoan era, were originally part of a mural decoration that may have graced the wall of a palace.

Gaming Board

10 A decorative gaming board, elaborately inlaid and decorated with rock crystal, gold and silver leaf, turquoise paste and ivory, shows that ancient Crete had a wealthy, leisured class, as well as trade links with other ancient civilizations.

Faience Figurines of the Snake Goddess

6 Unearthed at Knossos, these ornate ceramic figures display bare breasts, small waists and long flouncy skirts, and they carry a snake in either hand, as do some later depictions of the goddess Astarte. This has led some to suggest that there is continuity between ancient Crete and later Hellenic cultures. The figurines were discovered by Sir Arthur Evans (see p14), who considered them as possible evidence of a matriarchal society.

Jug of Reeds

7 With its dark pattern of reeds painted on a lighter background, this graceful pottery jug is the finest example of work from the New Palace era (1700–1450 BC).

An ancient, ornate gaming board

TOP 10 ★ Chania

Chania is Crete's prettiest (and second-largest) town, with colourful old Venetian buildings set around a sheltered harbour that is guarded by fortifications. To the south are the treeless peaks of the Lefka Ori (White Mountains), sometimes snow-covered until June. Good beaches lie to the west and on the Akrotiri peninsula to the east. As well as Venetian ramparts and churches, a handful of old Islamic buildings serve as reminders of the 250-year Ottoman rule.

1 Lighthouse
Walk out to the lighthouse at the tip of the Venetian harbour wall **(below)** for a fine view of the waterfront, harbour entrance and city.

Chania

3 Byzantine Collection
The collection, which rests in a 15th-century Venetian church, highlights Byzantine Crete, with coins, jewellery, statuary, mosaics and some fine icons.

4 Schiavo Bastion and Venetian Walls
The massive Schiavo Bastion and the high walls either side of it are the best-preserved elements of the landward section of the Venetian fortifications. They were built in the mid-15th century as the threat of Ottoman invasion loomed. Note that there is no public access.

2 Yali Tzami
The Turks erected this multi-domed mosque **(below)** to set their stamp on Crete after the conquest of 1645. The oldest Ottoman building on the island (also known as the Shore Mosque), it is now a gallery.

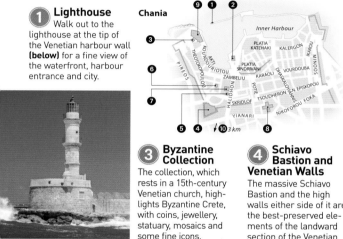

5 Cretan House Folklore Museum

With its fascinating collection of tools, looms and spinning wheels, plus colourful rugs, wall hangings and ornate embroidery, this lovely museum seeks to reveal and preserve traditional Cretan village skills *(see p51)*.

6 Etz Hayyim Synagogue

Chania's Jewish population used this 15th-century synagogue **(left)** until the German occupation of 1941–45, when they were deported to death camps. A plaque bears the names of the 276 Jews who died when a deportees' ship was inadvertently sunk by a British submarine.

7 Chania Archaeological Museum

The excellent collection here **(below)** includes Classical and Hellenistic sculpture and glassware, Minoan pottery and clay tablets, and some fine mosaics *(see p49)*.

8 Municipal Market

This covered market is best visited first thing in the morning. Local farm produce is piled high, and there is every imaginable variety of olive, herb and spice.

9 Firkas

Built to guard Chania harbour, this massive bastion now houses an eclectic Naval Museum, including a display depicting the Battle of Crete *(see p104)*.

CHANIA'S STORY

The first settlers were Minoans, who founded a powerful city named Kydonia on this site. The Romans overcame local resistance in 69 BC, and ruled from Kastelli hill. From 1252 until 1645, Chania mainly belonged to the Venetians. It fell to the Ottomans in 1645 and they remained until 1898. During World War II, civilians fought alongside Greek and Commonwealth troops.

10 "Oasis Beach"/ Kalamaki

Between the Chrissi Akti headland and Kalamaki, about 3 km (2 miles) west of the city centre, this is the best beach near Chania, with its long curve of sand and shingle, cafés and restaurants, and watersports.

NEED TO KNOW

MAP D2

Visitor Information: inside the town hall at Kydonias 29; 28213 41666; open 8:30am–2:30pm Mon–Sat

Firkas: open daily

Museums: open Tue–Sun

Market: open 7am–noon Mon–Sat

■ Chania is a great shopping centre. For beachwear and jewellery head to Chalidon and the harbour. Cretan-style leather boots are found in cobblers' shops on Skridlof.

■ The priciest eateries line the harbour esplanade. For cheaper food, try the streets of Splantzia district, east of Chalidon.

TOP 10 Phaistos

While Sir Arthur Evans was reconstructing Knossos, the more scientific Italian scholar Federico Halbherr was unearthing the sites of two Minoan palaces at Phaistos, on a hilltop above the farmlands of the Messara Plain. Most of the ruins visible today are remnants of a later palace (known as the Second Palace), built around 1600 BC and destroyed, possibly by a tidal wave, around 1450 BC.

1 Royal Apartments

Now fenced off, these rooms – the Queen's and the King's chambers, a covered pool, and even a bathroom and lavatory with running water – were the grandest in the complex **(below)**.

2 Grand Stairway

This broad stairway, the palace's main entrance, leads from the West Courtyard to the remains of a portico and into a colonnaded lightwell.

The ruins of the Minoan palace at Phaistos

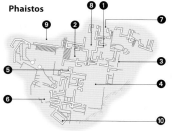

Phaistos

3 Palace Workshops

The remains of a bronzesmith's furnace or kiln stand in a courtyard. Nearby are small chambers – possibly workshops for the palace artisans.

4 Central Court

This vast courtyard, formerly flanked by covered walkways, may have been a parade ground. Niches, perhaps for sentries, are recessed into walls by the main entrance.

Previous pages View of Chania's multi-domed mosque from the harbour

5 Storerooms and Pithoi

The storerooms **(above)** were where essentials such as grain, oil, wine and olives were kept in huge ceramic jars called *pithoi*. Several *pithoi* remain on display.

6 First Palace Remains

To the southeast of the site, the smaller ruins of the First Palace are fenced off for their protection. The palace was built c.1900 BC and destroyed about 200 years later.

7 Archive

This neat row of mud-brick coffers may have been the filing department. This is where the Phaistos Disc, with its undeciphered hieroglyphics, was discovered. It is now on display in the Irakleio Archaeological Museum *(see pp18–19)*.

8 Peristyle Hall

The stumps of columns lining this square space indicate that it was once a colonnaded courtyard. Beneath it are traces of an even more archaic building, dating from what is known as the Prepalatial period (3000–1900 BC).

9 West Courtyard and Theatre Area

Several tiers of stone seats **(below)** occupy the north side of the West Courtyard, a paved space by the Minoans that was used for rituals and theatrical ceremonies, including, perhaps, the bull-vaulting depicted in some Minoan frescoes. South of the courtyard are two well-like stone-lined pits that were used for storing grain, and in the northeast corner are the remains of a shrine which was part of the earlier palace.

MINOAN DEMISE

There are many theories behind the sudden collapse of the Minoan civilization. Some believe it was the eruption of the volcano on the island of Kalliste (now Santorini), which would have triggered great tidal waves and clouds of volcanic ash. Other explanations include invasion by the warlike Mycenaeans of the mainland. However, all such theories remain speculative for now.

10 Classical Temple

The remnants of a small temple built during the Classical period and thought to be dedicated to Rhea, the mother of Zeus, provide evidence that the site at Phaistos was still inhabited more than 1,000 years after the mysterious collapse of the Minoan civilization about 3,500 years ago.

NEED TO KNOW

MAP H5 ■ 8 km (5 miles) W of Moires village ■ 28920 42315

Open 8am–8pm daily (winter: to 3pm); (last entry 7:45pm) closed some national holidays

Adm €8; Agia Triada free

■ The on-site Tourist Pavilion at Phaistos serves a range of cold drinks and food. However, you will find a much better taverna in the nearby village of Vori: Alekos Taverna, beside Agia Pelagia church.

■ For an overnight stop, head for the little resort of Matala, with sandy beaches and small hotels, less than 30 minutes' drive from Phaistos (see p93).

Rethymno

Rethymno, Crete's third-largest town, has been occupied since Minoan times and flourished under Venetian rule. Built on a wide, shallow bay, it has a good beach at the heart of town, and a medieval quarter crammed with the tall windows and wrought-iron balconies of old Venetian and Ottoman houses. Several well-preserved mosques (two of them former churches) remain from the Ottoman era, and, along with the palm trees planted along its seafront esplanade, they give the town a pleasantly exotic atmosphere.

Venetian Fortress (Fortezza)

Completed in 1580, this imposing stronghold **(right)** – one of the largest Venetian castles ever built – broods on a headland above the town. Within the walls, the most interesting building is the Ibrahim Han Mosque, which was originally the Venetian Cathedral *(see p47)*.

NEED TO KNOW

MAP F3

Visitor Information: Delfini Building, on Sofokli Venizelou; 28310 29148; open 8am–3pm Mon–Fri

Fortress: open 8:30am–8:30pm in summer; call 28310 28101 for winter hours; adm €4, family ticket €10, over 65s €3, children, students and disabled visitors free

Museums: Archaeological: open Tue–Sun; Folklore: open Mon–Sat Apr–Oct

■ Visit Rethymno early in July for the Cretan Diet Festival held in the Municipal Gardens.

■ The harbour front caters exclusively for tourists. Head to the old quarter's quieter alleys for cheaper, less crowded and more authentically Cretan restaurants.

Beach

Rethymno's town beach starts just east of the main harbour breakwater. Behind it is an esplanade lined with palm trees and an almost continuous chain of open-air cafés and restaurants.

Nerantzes Mosque (Odeion)

This Venetian church, now a conservatory **(right)**, was converted into a mosque by the Ottomans, who replaced the roof with cupolas and the bell tower with a balconied minaret. Today, the minaret is a true landmark in Rethymno.

Municipal Gardens

In summer, these gardens are a good place to escape the heat. The remains of an old Muslim cemetery here were covered by the gardens in 1924.

⑤ Rimondi Fountain

This fountain **(above)** was built in 1626 by one of Rethymno's patrician families. Both Venetians and Ottomans endowed cities with public fountains.

⑧ Rethymno Archaeological Museum

Opposite the main gate of the fortress, set in a converted Ottoman ravelin which served as the local jail until 1970, is the archaeological museum. Its displays **(below)** include finds from Neolithic, Minoan and Roman sites *(see p49)*.

Rethymno

⑩ Historical and Folk Art Museum

Vivid woven rugs and hangings, fine lace, traditional pottery, and silver and amber jewellery are among the relics of a vanished way of life preserved in this small museum. Richly decorated textiles from the Franzeskaki collection are displayed *(see p50)*.

⑥ Venetian Loggia (Lotzia)

The most important architectural reminder of Venice's long reign is now a shop selling museum-grade reproductions of Classical works of art.

⑨ Inner Harbour

Situated below the Venetian Fortress, Rethymno's small inner harbour is one of the most picturesque in Greece, with ramshackle old houses, small boats at anchor and a busy quayside **(below)**.

⑦ Venetian Gate (Porta Guora)

The only remnant of the city's Venetian fortifications is an arched stone gate, leading from the picturesque old quarter into the modern part of the city. Other gates were dismantled to provide better vehicle access.

TOP 10 ⭐ Gortys

The ruins of Gortys, in the middle of the fertile Messara Plain, date from a much later era than Crete's Minoan palaces. The large site, surrounded by trees, is less crowded than Crete's other top archaeological attractions, though it is just as impressive. It was probably first settled by the Minoans, but flourished later during the period of the Dorian city-states in the 6th century BC. In the 2nd century BC, Gortys defeated its rival Phaistos to become the leading Cretan city.

Basilica of Agios Titos ①

The impressive remains of the tree-aisled basilica **(right)** indicate that Christianity was already well established on the island by the 5th century, when the basilica was built. It is named after St Titus (Agios Titos), who welcomed St Paul the Apostle to Crete in AD 59 and became the first bishop of Crete.

③ Temple of Pythian Apollo

Believed to have been built during the 7th century BC, this temple had a monumental altar added in the Hellenistic period. It was converted into a Christian church during the 2nd century AD.

④ Roman Agora

A statue of the god of healing, Asclepius (now in the Irakleio Archaeological Museum), was discovered here. The agora, also known as the marketplace, was the heart of any ancient Greco-Roman city.

② Roman Odeion and Code of Laws

Built into the walls of a Roman odeion are a number of stone slabs inscribed with a code of laws **(above)**, dating from about 500 BC. These tablets are now regarded by scholars as the most significant archaeological feature at the Gortys site.

NEED TO KNOW

MAP J5 ▪ 1 km (half a mile) from Agioi Deka
▪ 28920 31144

Open 8am–8pm daily; last entry 7:45pm (winter: to 3pm); closed some national holidays

Adm €6; concessions €3

▪ Drive on to to Matala,

30 km (19 miles) southwest of Gortys, which has a fine sandy beach.

▪ Instead of using the spartan on-site cafeteria at Gortys, head for the nearby village of Agioi Deka, where there are pleasant tavernas and a historic church.

6 Praetorium

A courtyard and stumps of marble columns **(above)** are all that remain of the palace of the Roman governor of Crete and Libya.

7 Acropolis (Kastro)

Outside the main site, Roman ramparts and a small tower known as the Kastro ("castle") stand guard on a low hilltop. The site is fenced, and the worn-out path makes access difficult.

8 Museum

A collection of marble statuary unearthed at Gortys is on display in a small pavilion on site **(right)**, though many of the more impressive finds are held at the Irakleio Archaeological Museum *(see pp18–19)*.

10 Roman Baths

Remnants of the baths, which would have been a social hub of the Roman city, can be seen among olive groves south of the Praetorium.

9 Minoan Rural Villa

West of the Metropolianos stream, lie the excavated remains of a Minoan villa **(below)** with 30 rooms dating from the Neopalatial Period (1700–1450 BC).

Gortys

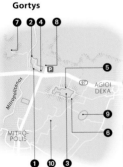

5 Temple of Isis and Serapis

Ancient Crete had links with ancient Egypt, as shown by the remains of this temple, dedicated to the Egyptian deities.

🔟 ⭐ Samaria Gorge

The Samaria Gorge, which cuts its way through the Lefka Ori (White Mountains) from the Omalos Plateau to the Libyan Sea, is one of the most striking areas of natural beauty in Greece. Peaks soar on both sides of the gorge, flanked by pine woods and wildflower meadows. Beginning 1,250 m (4,100 ft) above sea level, it emerges on the coast, close to the little village of Agia Roumeli, after passing through the narrow Sideresportes or "Iron Gates".

4 Old Agia Roumeli

A ruined Venetian-era church and a few cottages are all that remain of this old village. On the left (east) bank of the gorge exit lie the ruins of ancient Tarra; up the hill, beyond the right bank sits a crumbled Ottoman fortress.

1 Xyloskalo

The zig zag path **(above)** down through the gorge is called the Xyloskalo. The toughest part plummets a breathtaking 1,000 m (3,280 ft) in little more than 2 km (1 mile), passing through pine and cypress woods.

2 Church of Agios Nikolaos

Not far from the foot of the Xyloskalo and the springs, the tiny chapel of Agios Nikolaos **(below)** stands in the shade of pine and cypress trees, next to a rest area.

3 Gingilos and Volakias Peaks

Above the Xyloskalo path to the southwest, the skyline is dominated by the massive peaks of Gingilos (2,080 m/6,824 ft) and Volakias (2,116 m/6,942 ft). It is not unusual for these mountaintops to remain snow covered well into the early summer, even when the temperatures at sea level are scorching.

Samaria Gorge

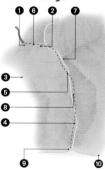

NEED TO KNOW

MAP C4 ■ Forest Guardhouse, Xyloskalo; 28210 67179 ■ Forest Guardhouse, Agia Roumeli; 28250 91254

Open May–mid-Oct (weather permitting, phone first to check): 7am–8pm daily

Adm €5; keep your date-stamped ticket, which you must hand in at the Agia Roumeli gate as you leave

■ Though fit walkers can complete the 17-km (11-mile) trek in about 5 hours, it is best to allow 8, including a break of at least an hour. Rest during the hottest part of the day in summer.

■ Take at least one litre of water per person. There are rest areas where you can picnic in the shade, and at Agia Roumeli there are several tavernas for your recuperation.

GETTING AROUND

Several companies run guided walks, which include transport to and from the gorge. There are also buses from Chania to Omalos, 1 km (half a mile) from Xyloskalo. Independent walkers must report to the Forest Guardhouse at Xyloskalo before setting out. There are many guesthouses in Agia Roumeli.

8 Osia Maria
Dwarfed by steep cliffs, this small church contains 14th-century frescoes and lends its name to the gorge itself.

9 New Agia Roumeli
The inhabitants of Agia Roumeli abandoned their village in the 1960s, intent on a new location by the sea **(below)**. The new village has grown into a string of tavernas and guesthouses spread out along a single street.

5 Sideresportes
Near the shrine of Afendis Christos, the gorge narrows to just 3 m (9 ft) of space separating rocky walls that rise 700 m (more than 2,000 ft) **(above)**.

6 Neroutsiko and Riza Sykias
The bubbling springs of Neroutsiko and Riza Sykias meet at the foot of the Xyloskalo path. During winter, they form a fierce torrent that makes the gorge impassable, but in the summer months, they dry to a trickle.

7 Samaria
The last dwellers in the gorge abandoned this village in 1962, when the area was designated a national park. The ghostly cottages have become ever more derelict over time.

10 Agios Pavlos Beach
An hour's walk east of Agia Roumeli, Agios Pavlos beach is a long stretch of sand and pebbles with a taverna. It is named after the tiny chapel here, dedicated to St Paul.

TOP 10 ★ The Amari Valley and Mount Idi

The remote Amari Valley, overlooked by Mount Idi, is one of Crete's most scenic areas, dotted with churches, olive groves and vineyards. Surprisingly fertile thanks to topsoil washed from surrounding slopes, this region was among the wealthiest in Crete in the Byzantine era. During World War II, many of its villages were destroyed by the Germans in retaliation for attacks by the resistance, and its kidnapping of General Kreipe.

1 Thronos
The 11th-century church of the Panagia at Thronos holds frescoes and traces of ancient mosaics. A nearby shop keeps the church keys.

3 Agios Ioannis Theologos
The 13th-century church of St John the Divine sits by the road just north of Kardaki village. The frescoes date from 1347.

4 Ideou Cave
According to Greek myth, Zeus was raised in this enormous cavern, 20 minutes' walk from the Nida Plateau. In ancient times, this was a place of pilgrimage. Artifacts such as bronze shields, left as offerings to Zeus in the 8th century BC, are found in the Irakleio Archaeological Museum. The cavern is open daily.

5 Kamares Cave
This cave, where remarkable Minoan pottery known as Kamares ware was discovered, is a 4-hour trek from Kamares village. This sacred site was dedicated to the goddess Eileithyia.

2 Moni Asomaton
The monastery of Asomaton **(above)**, built during the Venetian era, is now deserted. It stands in an oasis of plane trees, palms and eucalyptus.

Panoramic view over the lush Amari Valley

8 Amari Village

A Venetian clock tower (**left**) is one of the older buildings in the valley. Just outside the village, some of Crete's oldest Christian frescoes, dated 1225, are in Agia Anna church.

9 The Memorial to Peace

German artist Karen Raeck's work, to the north of the Nida Plateau, is a winged figure outlined in huge natural stone boulders.

GETTING AROUND THE VALLEY

Though the Amari Valley feels remote, there is one bus running on weekdays (Mon–Fri) from Rethymno to the region's two largest villages, Thronos and Amari. With a hired car, it is possible to drive up one side of the valley and down the other. Of the two roads going through the valley, the eastern route is the most spectacular.

The Amari Valley and Mount Idi

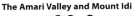

6 Hromonastiri

The church of Agios Efstathios, outside Hromonastiri village, contains frescoes dating from the 11th century, which may be the oldest of their kind in Crete.

10 Fourfouras

A pretty village set in mountain scenery, Fourfouras is one of the jumping-off spots for the ascent of Mount Idi and some of the less challenging hikes on the Psiloritis massif.

7 Mount Idi (Psiloritis) Summit

Towering above the valley, the 2,456-m (8,060-ft) peak of Mt Idi, also called Ida and Psiloritis, is the highest mountain in Crete (**below**). Marked walking trails (see p64) lead to the top from the Nida Plateau, 23 km (14 miles) by road from Anogeia village.

NEED TO KNOW

MAP G–H4

Greek National Tourism Organization: Delfini Building, Sofokli Venizelou, Rethymno; 28310 29148

■ Amari is a good base from which to explore the valley and surrounding mountains on foot. There are several tavernas and rooms to rent. Alternately, try the nearby village of Spili, directly west over the Kedros range.

■ Guided fossil-hunting and herb-gathering walks (€30 per person) around the Amari Valley are organized by Lambros Papoutsakis in Thronos village (28330 22760). Another walk takes participants to Psiloritis summit, starting before dawn (€50 per person).

TOP 10 ★ Gournia

Unearthed by the American archaeologist Harriet Boyd Hawes between 1901 and 1904, Gournia is the best-preserved Minoan town in Crete, though it receives few visitors. Its layout, with narrow stepped streets and tiny houses, is surprisingly similar to that of modern-day Cretan villages. It is also one of the oldest sites, inhabited from around 3000 BC, though the surviving buildings date from the later Second Palace Period. Like other Minoan settlements, it was destroyed by earthquake and fire around 1450 BC. The honeycomb of ruins stands only waist high.

1 Carpenter's Workshop

Tools and other materials found in this small building indicate that it was used by a woodworker who may also have lived on the premises with his family.

Ruins of the ancient Minoan settlement of Gournia

2 Stairway

The L-shaped stair **(above)** that rises from the courtyard to the central court of the palace is characteristic of Minoan palaces. Its design echoes similar ceremonial stairs found in virtually every Minoan palace site in Crete.

3 Central Palace Court

Access to the central court of the palace from the courtyard below is by the ceremonial staircase. The Minoan ruler of Gournia may well have used this antechamber to the small palace building as his audience hall.

4 Shrine

A cobbled, mosaic-decorated path leads steeply up to a small shrine, which was found to contain cult objects. The terracotta goddess figurines and snake are now displayed in the Irakleio Archaeological Museum *(see pp18–19)*.

NEED TO KNOW

MAP P5 ▪ S of coast road, 18 km (11 miles) E of Agios Nikolaos ▪ 28420 93028

Open 8am–3pm Tue–Sun

Adm €3

▪ **Unfortunately, the beaches near Gournia are not very appealing.**

▪ **There is nowhere to eat at Gournia. Pachia Ammos, 3 km (2 miles) east, has a string of waterfront restaurants.**

6 Palace

Gournia's palace (above), which may have been the dwelling place of a governor who ruled Gournia on behalf of the Minoan ruler of Knossos, is a miniature version of the more important Minoan royal palaces. In the centre of the palace stands what is believed to be a sacrificial altar.

7 Storerooms

Adjoining the palace is a series of storerooms, or magazines, where grain, oil and other essentials would have once been stored in large earthenware jars.

LOST NAMES

Although some Minoan scripts have now been deciphered, scholars and archaeologists still have no way of knowing what the Minoans called most of their cities. The names by which they are known today stem from words that were used by the much later Greek settlers who occupied the island long after the collapse of Minoan civilization.

9 Bronzesmith's Workshop

Bronze nails and scraps, and a simple stone anvil suggest a smithy used in smelting bronze. Tools, weapons, utensils and votive objects from Gournia are now on display at the Irakleio Archaeological Museum.

10 Potter's Workshop

Clay fragments indicate this was a potter's workshop (below). The finds unearthed in this and other buildings indicate Gournia was suddenly abandoned rather than slowly run down.

Gournia

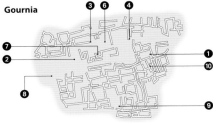

5 Wash Basins

The stone basins found outside most buildings in Gournia are known as *gournes* in modern Greek. Archaeologists named the long-lost site after them.

8 Courtyard

At the southern end of the site, an expansive courtyard may have been the town's market. It was probably also used for ceremonial purposes.

🔟 ⭐ Moni Arkadiou

High above Crete's north coast, on a fertile plain at the base of Mount Idi, Moni Arkadiou (Arkadi Monastery) dates from the 16th century. When Crete fell under Ottoman occupation in 1669, monasteries became important centres of resistance – thanks, in part, to their isolation. Besides teaching Christian values, the monks kept alive the Greek language, and during Crete's many 18th- and 19th-century rebellions, Orthodox priests often led freedom fighters into combat. Despite Arkadi's serene atmosphere, it conceals a tragic story, and the Cretan independence movement slogan "Freedom or Death" (today the Greek national motto) holds special significance here.

Monastery Church

This Venetian-Baroque church **(right)** dates from 1587. The humble interior has whitewashed walls, two altars, golden candelabras, icons covered by silver plating (so that just the saints' faces are visible) and flickering votive candles.

② Courtyard Garden

The courtyard **(below)** is lined with fragrant roses. Stone pillars support a pergola draped with vines, while terracotta pots hold geraniums and bougainvillea, and cats snooze in the shade of a cypress tree.

③ Museum

The monastery refectory now hosts a museum, with exhibits including ecclesiastical books and manuscripts, holy crosses, silk vestments embroidered with golden thread and religious icons. Look out for *St John the Baptist* and *Christ Enthroned*.

⑤ Gunpowder Store

This building is where, on 8 November 1866, 943 Cretan martyrs blew themselves up rather than surrender to the Ottomans. Today, a commemorative plaque reads: "The flame which lights the depths of this crypt was a Godly flame in which the Cretans perished for freedom."

④ Arkadi Café

Next to the memorial, the café serves drinks and snacks at tables on a shaded terrace with views over the surrounding countryside. There is also a children's playground with swings and a slide.

7 Monks' Cells

Throughout the 17th century, about 100 monks resided here – today there are only three left. Behind the church, you can see a couple of the former monks' cells – small and simply furnished **(left)**.

8 Memorial to the Dead

Outside the monastery complex, a five-minute walk brings you to a raised stone terrace shaded by pine trees. Here, inside a former windmill, hexagonal in plan, an ossuary displays the skulls of those who perished during the Arkadi Holocaust of 1866.

9 Outer Walls

The monastery was fortified in the 16th century to defend it against attack and to offer refuge to both the monks and the local community. Visitors can enter through the main portal, an arched gateway in the west facade, from 1870.

THE ARKADI HOLOCAUST

On 8 November 1866, the monastery came under siege by the Ottoman army. Some 700 women and children (who had sought refuge within its walls) and over 200 Cretan freedom fighters barricaded themselves inside. Rather than surrender, they fired their store of gunpowder, blowing themselves (and many attackers) up. This act of defiance was the culmination of five revolts since 1770. Crete was finally united with Greece in 1913.

10 Dead Tree

As you face the church facade, you will see a cypress and an olive tree. Behind them, the dead tree **(below)** has a bullet from the 1866 siege still embedded in its trunk.

6 Refectory

A gate located opposite the iconic dead tree leads into a second – smaller and more peaceful – courtyard. Cross this space to arrive at the refectory, a long, narrow space with a vaulted ceiling. The monks would dine together here, sitting at communal wooden tables.

NEED TO KNOW

MAP G4 ■ Arkadi, 23 km (14 miles) SE of Rethymno
■ 28310 83135

Open 9am–8pm Mon–Sat, 10am–8pm Sun (winter: to an hour before sunset)

Adm €3

■ Buses depart daily from Rethymno KTEL (10am and 1pm, returning 12:15 and 3:15pm; journey time 40 mins). Alternatively, a miniature train follows the same route.

■ On 8 November each year, a 1-minute silence is held at the monastery to mark the Arkadi Holocaust, and a commemorative ceremony takes place in the monastery church.

■ Arkadi Monastery featured on the now retired 100 drachma banknote.

The Top 10 of Everything

Vibrant mural decorations inside the palace of Knossos

Moments in History

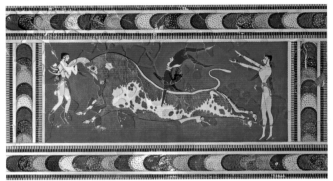

Fresco from the palace of Knossos showing an acrobat leaping over a bull

1 1750 BC: Golden Age of Minoan Culture

Crete is the centre of the Minoan civilization, which is marked by the building of Knossos and other grand palaces. Mycenaeans take over Knossos shortly after 1450 BC.

2 Roman Conquest

The first Roman invasion of Crete in 71 BC is repulsed by the Dorian Greeks, but a second attack in 69 BC succeeds. Some Cretan cities side with the invaders, and by 67 BC, Crete is firmly in Roman hands.

3 Byzantine Reconquest

The Byzantine Empire loses Crete to Arab invaders in AD 824.

Emperor Nikephoros Phokas

Just over a century later, in 961, General Nikephoros Phokas reconquers the island.

4 Venetian Rule

Crete falls into Venetian hands shortly after 1204, when the Fourth Crusade goes awry and the Byzantine emperor is deposed by an army of Frankish crusaders in alliance with Venice. Cretans rebel against the Venetians, but without success.

5 The Ottoman Turks

Chania and Rethymno fall to an attack by Turks in 1645. Venetian sea power enables the Venetian capital of Candia (modern Irakleio) to resist a 21-year siege, but Venice finally surrenders in 1669. The Cretans revolt repeatedly against the Ottomans. The first major rebellion, led by Ioannis Daskalogiannis, erupts in Sfakia in 1770. It is crushed, with Sfakia subdued for the first time.

6 War of Independence

In 1821, a nationwide uprising in mainland Greece becomes a full-scale War of Independence. In Crete, Chatzimichalis Dalianis and 385 rebels occupy Frangokastello in May 1828, where they are slaughtered. Mehmet Ali of Egypt had already pacified most of Crete, which remains Ottoman.

7 Rebellions Against Cretan Muslims

Undaunted by further heroic failures in 1841 and 1858, Crete rises again in 1866, with a self-appointed Cretan Assembly declaring independence and union with Greece. The Ottomans import Egyptian troops to quell the rebels, but in Europe there is growing sympathy for the Cretan cause.

8 Great Powers Intervene

Further revolts in 1889 and 1896 culminate in the landing of Greek troops in 1897 as well as intervention by France, Britain, Russia and Italy. Crete becomes semi-autonomous, ruled by a Christian-Muslim assembly, chaired by Prince George of Greece.

An uprising in the late 19th century

9 Union with Greece

In 1905, local politician Eleftherios Venizelos convenes a revolutionary assembly, which in 1908 unilaterally declares *enosis* (union) with Greece. This does not occur until 1913.

10 Occupation and Liberation in World War II

German forces drive the Allies out of Crete in May 1941, but Cretan guerrillas continue to resist. Most German troops flee Greece in October 1944 as Allied troops land, but the garrison at Chania holds out until Berlin falls in May 1945.

TOP 10 EMPIRES AND GOVERNMENTS

Picture of an Ottoman seige

1 Minoan Empires
The Minoan civilization emerged between 3000 and 1900 BC. A volcanic explosion may have destroyed the Minoan cities around 1450 BC.

2 Mycenaeans
Mycenaean Greeks from the mainland settled in Crete after 1450 BC.

3 The Dorians
During the 1100s, Dorian Greeks from northern Greece drove the descendants of the Minoans into remote areas.

4 Dorian City-States
Gortys and Kydonia (modern Chania) were among the most powerful.

5 Roman Empire
Gortys (which had sided with invading Rome) became capital of the province of Crete and Cyrenaica.

6 Byzantine Empire
In the 4th century AD, Crete became part of the Byzantine realm.

7 Arab Conquest and Retreat
From AD 824–961, Arab forces led by the Andalucian Abu Hafs occupied Crete; Byzantine general Nikephoros Phokas expelled them.

8 Venetian Empire
In 1210, the Republic of Venice took control of Crete in the wake of the Fourth Crusade.

9 Ottoman Empire
The Ottoman Turks invaded Crete in strength in 1645 and held the island until the end of the 19th century.

10 Kingdom of the Hellenes
Crete was united with Greece in 1913. From 1898 to 1923, around 100,000 Muslim Cretans voluntarily departed, or were expelled.

TOP 10 Ancient Sites

1 Itanos
MAP R4 ■ 2 km (1 mile) N of Vai ■ Unenclosed

The remains of a Hellenistic wall, foundations of two early Christian basilicas, and toppled columns are the only indications that this was once an important city. It flourished until early medieval times, when it was destroyed by Saracen raiders.

Ruins of the basilica, Itanos

2 Gournia
The well-preserved remains of the Minoan town of Gournia, a maze of roofless stone walls, makes an interesting contrast with the better-known Minoan palaces. This was a working community, and archaeologists discovered workshops used by potters, smiths and carpenters, alongside tiny houses surrounding a small palace (see pp34–5).

3 Agia Triada
A treasury of Minoan relics, including tablets inscribed with the still undeciphered Minoan Linear A script, has been discovered on this site of a Minoan villa, built about 1700 BC. The site was later occupied by Mycenaean settlers, who built a megaron (chief's hall) and a village with a unique row of porticoed shops (see p90).

4 Malia
MAP M4 ■ 3 km (2 miles) E of Malia ■ 28970 31597 ■ 8am–5pm Tue–Sun ■ Adm

East of the busy summer holiday resort of Malia is the archaeological site of the same name. The Minoan double-axe symbol, or labrys, is carved into two pillars of a small shrine, which forms part of the remains of a palace dating circa 1600 BC. Excavations are still going on near the palace site.

5 Zakros
MAP R5 ■ Kato Zakros ■ 28430 26897 ■ 8am–6pm daily ■ Adm

The fourth-largest of Crete's Minoan palaces, Zakros was rediscovered in 1961 by the Cretan archaeologist Nikolaos Platon. The site had not been plundered, and finds included a stunning rock crystal jug, which is today housed in the Irakleio Archaeological Museum (see pp18–19). Remains of the palace and a cistern can be seen.

6 Praisos

MAP Q5 ■ By Nea Praisos village ■ Unenclosed

This scenic site – with only the remnants of a temple, house foundations and a city wall to be seen – was the last enclave of the Eteocretan ("true Cretan") descendants of the Minoans. It survived until the 2nd century BC.

7 Levin

MAP J6 ■ N of Lendas ■ Unenclosed

Ancient Levin, on a hilltop just outside the modern village of Lendas, is now no more than a scattering of ruined walls and pillars around a stone arch. The site was a sanctuary dedicated to Asclepius, the god of healing. From the 3rd century BC until the Christian era, it was an important place of pilgrimage.

8 Phaistos

The ruins of the Minoan palace at Phaistos, on a hilltop by the south coast of Crete, are second only to those at Knossos. A maze of walls and courtyards marks the site of the Second Palace at Phaistos, built around 1600 BC. Hieroglyphics on the clay Phaistos Disc still puzzle scientists today (see pp24–5).

Remains of the basilica at Gortys

9 Gortys

The ruined city of Gortys, with the basilica of Agios Titos and remnants of a Roman provincial governor's palace, dates from the early Christian era. The site extends over quite a wide area, and is usually uncrowded, so it can be explored at leisure (see pp28–9).

The Phaistos Disc, carved with symbols

10 Knossos

Just outside Irakleio, Knossos is by far the most striking of the Minoan palace ruins on Crete. Dating back more than 3,500 years, it was destroyed in around 1450 BC, probably by a combination of volcanic eruption and invaders, and not rediscovered until the late 19th century (see pp12–15).

The imposing palace of Knossos

🔟 Churches and Monasteries

Interior of Panagia Kera at Krista

adm) is also worth visiting for its older architecture and another museum.

③ Agia Pelagia
Open access

This tiny 14th-century church, well-signposted near the top of this village, has quirky frescoes of the life of Christ such as *His Presentation to the Crucifixion*, as well as assorted saints and even musicians.

④ Agios Nikolaos
MAP D2 ▪ 8am–7pm daily

This church has a history that reflects Chania's past. It was built by the Venetians, converted into a mosque after the Ottoman conquest, and in the early 20th century, it was converted again into a Greek Orthodox church dedicated to St Nicholas. Its minaret is a relic from the centuries of Muslim worship here.

① Panagia Kera
MAP N5 ▪ 28410 51525
▪ 8am–3pm Tue–Sun ▪ Adm

Crete's main Byzantine-era church, Panagia Kera was built in the 13th and 14th centuries. It is adorned with vivid, unusual frescoes, many of them from the apocryphal gospels, as well as a rare Orthodox depiction of Catholic saint Francis.

② Moni Preveli
MAP F5 ▪ 28320 31246
▪ 9am–6:30pm daily ▪ Adm

Built during the 17th century to replace a nearby monastery, Moni Piso Preveli's cells overlook a broad, open courtyard to the Libyan sea. It has a church and a small museum where exhibits include ornamented vestments, church silver and icons. Kato Prevelli (same hours,

⑤ Moni Arkadiou
Though founded in the 5th century, most of this monastic complex dates from the 16th century. Moni Arkadiou has a special meaning for Cretans. During the great revolt of 1866, the monastery – crowded with refugees and freedom fighters – was besieged by Cretan Muslims. Rather than surrender, the rebel defenders blew up their gunpowder stores, killing themselves and many of their enemies (see pp36–7).

Church façade, Moni Arkadiou

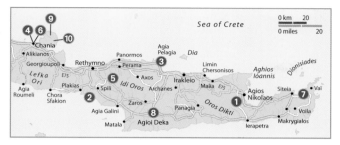

⑥ Moni Chrissopygis
MAP D2 ▪ 28210 91125
▪ 8am–noon & 3:30–6pm daily ▪ Adm

The Convent of the Golden Font (Life-Giving Spring), dates from the late Venetian era but has been rebuilt many times, most recently in 1976. The nuns paint icons using traditional methods.

Byzantine icon at Moni Toplou

⑦ Moni Toplou
MAP R4 ▪ 28430 61226
▪ 9am–1pm & 2–6pm daily ▪ Adm

Fortified against bandits at its 14th-century foundation, Toplou monastery features a forbidding exterior. Inside, however, is a different world of serene, flower-filled courtyards and cloisters, and a church that houses the icon *Lord, Thou Art Great* by Ioannis Kornaros.

⑧ Agioi Deka Church
MAP J5 ▪ 8am–5pm

This 13th-century Byzantine Church of the Ten Saints stands on the spot where ten Cretan Christians were martyred by the troops of the Roman Emperor Decius in AD 250. A striking icon depicting the ten saints with golden halos is displayed in the nave.

⑨ Moni Katholiko
MAP D2 ▪ Open access

In a valley riddled with caves once used by hermits, the abandoned monastery of Katholiko is a ghostly place, with crumbling buildings that seem to have grown out of the rock face.

⑩ Moni Agia Triada Tzangarolon
MAP D2 ▪ 28210 63572 ▪ 9am–7pm daily (Museum Hall closed Sun) ▪ Adm

Tzangarolon monastery stands among its own olive groves. Although its monastic community has dwindled to just a few members, its old buildings are gradually being restored and its church exterior vies with Arkadiou for ornateness. Visitors are welcome, and the monks will sell you high-quality, home-grown olive oil and wine.

Iconostasis at Moni Agia Triada

🔟 Venetian Castles

1 Frangokastello
MAP E4

The Venetians built this fortress to defend the south coast from Saracen pirates. In May 1828 it was occupied by Greek insurgents, who were massacred by a much larger Muslim force. Yearly, around the battle anniversary, legend has it that the defeated appear as phantoms marching out of nearby sand dunes. The repaired castle hosts summer events (see p55 & p102).

The coastal fortress of Frangokastello

2 Venetian Tower, Finikas, Loutro
MAP D4

The lonely tower, standing on a headland between Loutro and the bay of Finix, is yet another Venetian relic. Nearby are a few scattered blocks, the remains of a Byzantine church and also a Hellenistic town, the latter an important seaport when the Romans ruled Crete.

3 Chania
MAP D2

The Venetians lost Chania to their arch-rivals, the Genoese, in 1263. They regained it 22 years later, and set about making the town impregnable, starting with walls around the hill above the harbour in the district still known as Kastelli (the castle). Further walls followed, but though they may have deterred occasional pirate raids, they proved entirely ineffective when the Ottomans assailed the city in 1645.

4 Paleochora
MAP B4

Kastel Selinou, as Paleochora was first known, was built in 1279 to guard the southwest against pirates. The great Muslim corsair Barbarossa destroyed it in 1539. The Ottomans saw no need to rebuild it, and Paleochora fort has remained an elegant ruin ever since.

5 Da Molini Castle Ruins, Alikianos
MAP C2

Though much overgrown, the dilapidated walls standing among clutches of citrus trees are still impressive. The castle was the scene of a notorious massacre, when the early 16th-century Cretan rebel leader Georgios Kandanoleon was betrayed by Francesco Molini during his son's wedding to Molini's daughter.

Siteia's imposing Venetian fortress

6 Venetian Fortress, Siteia
MAP Q4

This restored fort is all that remains of the city's once substantial ring of battlements, which resisted a siege by the Ottomans in 1648–51. It is now used as an open-air theatre for concerts and plays in summer.

7 Gramvousa
MAP B1

In around 1220, the Venetians built a strong fortress on this tiny islet off northwestern Crete, and – along with fortified Spinalonga and Souda islets – held it until 1715, long after they had lost Crete itself. Boat excursions are available from Kissamos.

8 Venetian Acropolis and Ancient Polyrrinia
MAP B2

On a hilltop above modern Polyrrinia village, a Venetian keep shares the peak with the ruins of Hellenistic Polyrrinia, which thrived until the Andalucian Arab invasion of the 9th century. Stone from Hellenistic buildings, already 1,000 years old when the Venetians arrived, has been incorporated into the castle walls.

9 Rethymno Fortezza

The massive fortress that dominates Rethymno's harbour was built by the Venetians with sloping walls to better deflect the Ottoman Empire's gigantic cannon. But it proved no match for the military ingenuity of the Ottomans, who simply skirted it when they took the city in 1645. The Fortezza never again had a military function, and until recently many houses nestled within (see also p26).

The mosque inside Rethymno's Fortezza

10 Spinalonga

This formidable island fortress was built in 1579 to command the entrance to the Gulf of Mirabello. Venice managed to keep it after the surrender of Candia (Irakleio) in 1669, and relinquished it by treaty in 1715. From 1903, it was used for a time as a leper colony, as told in Victoria Hislop's novel The Island (see p111).

The fortress of Spinalonga, overlooking Elounda Bay

🔟 Art and Archaeological Museums

1 Archanes Collection

MAP K4 ▪ Kalochristianaki, Archanes ▪ 2810 752712 ▪ Summer: 8am–3pm Wed–Mon

Finds from the Minoan cemetery discovered at Fourni, just north of Archanes village, are displayed in this small archaeological museum, along with relics from other nearby sites.

2 Museum of Contemporary Art, Rethymno

MAP F3 ▪ Himaras 5, Rethymno 74100 ▪ 28310 52530 ▪ May–Oct: 9am–2pm & 7–9pm Tue–Fri, 10am–3pm Sat & Sun; Nov–Apr: 9am–2pm Tue–Fri, 6–9pm Wed & Fri, 10am–3pm Sat & Sun ▪ Adm

This museum has around 500 works by local artist L Kanakakis, as well as works by other leading, contemporary Greek artists. The pieces range from the 1950s to the present day. It also holds temporary exhibitions, as well as classes and workshops, open to the public.

3 Irakleio Archaeological Museum

Besides its most famous Minoan exhibits, the collection here includes significant Roman-era finds. *(see pp18–19)*.

4 Historical Museum of Crete

MAP S1 ▪ Sofokli Venizelou 27, Irakleio ▪ 2810 283219 ▪ Apr–Oct: 9am–5pm Mon–Sat (Nov–Mar: to 3:30pm) ▪ Adm

Wonderfully eclectic displays include an interactive model of the medieval town, two genuine El Grecos, rescued icons and frescoes, as well as antiquarian prints from World War II and the city of Irakleio.

Statuette, Irakleio Archaeological Museum

5 Archaeological Museum of Kissamos

MAP B2 ▪ Plateia Tzanaki ▪ 28220 83308 ▪ 8:30am–3pm Tue–Sun ▪ Adm

Housed in a fine Venetian-Turkish building, this museum displays Hellenistic and Roman artifacts, including jewellery, statues and two exquisite mosaic floors.

Floor mosaic in the Archaeological Museum of Kissamos

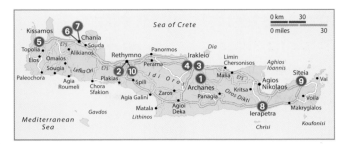

Chania Archaeological Museum

8 Ierapetra Archaeological Museum

MAP N6 ■ 1 Kostoula Adrianou Ierapetra ■ 28420 28721 ■ 9am–3pm Tue–Sun ■ Adm

Exhibits inside this former Muslim academy include huge clay storage jars (pithoi), Minoan clay sarcophagi (larnakes) statues, bronze weapons and tools dating from the time of the Dorian city-states, when Ierapetra became one of the most powerful cities in eastern Crete.

6 Chania Archaeological Museum

MAP B6 ■ 28210 90334 ■ 8am–3pm Tue–Sun ■ Disabled access ■ Adm

Set in a former Venetian church, later an Ottoman mosque, this museum is filled with Minoan finds, Hellenistic and Roman marble sculpture, pottery and jewellery found at archaeological sites in western Crete.

9 Siteia Archaeological Museum

MAP Q4 ■ Fiskokefalou 3 ■ 28430 23917 ■ 8am–3pm Tue–Sun ■ Adm

The main exhibits are from the palace site at Zakros, on Crete's east coast, which was uncovered in 1961. They include clay tablets inscribed with the symbols of the Minoan Linear A script, as well as bronze and kitchen tools.

Vase, Siteia Archaeological Museum

7 Byzantine Collection of Chania

MAP A5 ■ 78 Theotokopoulou ■ 28210 96046 ■ 8am–3pm Tue–Sun ■ Adm

The fine collection of Cretan icons is the best reason to visit this small museum next to Chania's harbour fortress, housed in the Venetian church of San Salvatore. The collection also features a floor mosaic, fresco fragments rescued from country chapels, jewellery, ceramics and coins.

10 Rethymno Archaeological Museum

MAP P1 ■ Himaras, Fortetza ■ 28310 54668 ■ 8am–3pm Tue–Sun ■ Adm

In a converted ravelin built by the Ottomans, this museum's collection stretches from the Stone Age to Minoan and Hellenistic eras. Finds from archaeological sites and caves in the Rethymno area include late Minoan painted burial caskets, or larnakes, and goods found in Minoan cemetery sites.

ᴛᴏᴘ10 Cretan Cultural Museums

Lychnostatis Open Air Museum

1 Lychnostatis Open Air Museum of Folk Culture

MAP M4 ▪ Chersonisos ▪ 28970 23660 ▪ Apr–Nov: 9am–2pm Sun–Fri; winter: visits by appt ▪ Adm ▪ www.lychnostatis.gr

Traditional Cretan ways of life began to die out in recent decades. This open-air museum gives some insight into life on the island before tourism, TVs and mobile phones. Exhibits include a windmill and an old stone cottage.

2 Historical and Folk Art Museum, Rethymno

MAP P2 ▪ Vernardou 28-30 ▪ 28310 23398 ▪ 10am–2:30pm Mon–Sat; may close Nov–Mar ▪ Adm

This converted Venetian mansion displays relics of a vanished way of life, including colourful woven artifacts, embroidery, farm and kitchen implements, and ceramics.

3 Olive Tree Museum, Vouves

MAP C2 ▪ Ano Vouves (30 km/19 miles W of Chania) ▪ www.olivemuseumvouves.com

Set amid olive groves, with one tree said to be 3,000 years old, this quaint museum traces the history of olive oil. Exhibits include an old press and terracotta pots. The adjoining café serves delicious cakes.

4 Agios Nikolaos Folklore Museum

MAP N4 ▪ Kondylaki 2 ▪ 28410 25093 ▪ May–Oct: 9:30am–1:30pm & 5–9pm ▪ Adm

Overlooking Agios Nikolaos's lagoon-like inner harbour, the Folklore Museum houses colourful textiles and costumes, plus farming and fishing equipment.

5 Arolithos Museum of Agricultural History and Popular Art

MAP K4 ▪ Arolithos village, 8 km/5 miles W of Irakleio on old highway ▪ 2810 821050 ▪ Apr–Oct: 9am–3pm, Nov–Mar: by appt ▪ Adm ▪ www.arolithos.com

This museum is linked with a holiday village which tries to give its guests a taste of traditional Cretan life, with craft workers, plus a restaurant and bakery with wood-burning ovens.

6 War Museum of Askifou

MAP E4 ▪ Askifou ▪ 6979 149719 ▪ 8am–8pm daily ▪ Donations welcome ▪ www.warmuseumaskifou.com

This museum was founded by George Hatzidakis, who wanted to collect every vestige of the Cretan struggle between 1941–44. Today, the collection has over 2,000 items.

Memorabilia, War Museum of Askifou

7 Cretan House Folklore Museum, Chania

MAP B6 ▪ 46B Chalidon ▪ 28210 90816
▪ 8am–3pm & 6–9pm Mon–Sat ▪ Adm

Traditional looms and spinning wheels, richly coloured rugs, wall hangings and embroidery can be found at this delightful place.

8 Museum of Cretan Ethnology, Vori

MAP H5 ▪ Vori ▪ 28920 91110 ▪ Apr–Oct: 11am–5pm daily; closed winter except for groups by appt ▪ Adm ▪ www.cretanethnologymuseum.gr

Two floors of displays elucidate by-gone rural life with tools relating to everything from pig-butchering to boot-making and eel trapping. There is also furniture and ironwork.

Vori's Museum of Cretan Ethnology

9 Verekinthos Arts and Crafts Village

MAP D2 ▪ Souda ▪ www.verekinthos.com

This formerly abandoned village near Souda port has been regenerated as an arts-and-crafts centre. With some 25 workshops hosting glassmakers, silversmiths, potters and weavers, it is a great place to shop for souvenirs.

10 Historical and Folklore Museum of Gavalochori

MAP E3 ▪ Gavalochori village ▪ 28250 23222 ▪ Apr–Oct: 10am–8pm Mon–Sat, 11am–6pm Sun ; Nov–Mar: 8:30am–3pm ▪ Adm

This excellent small museum in an old Venetian-Ottoman mansion depicts the history and culture of the village. Highlights include local skills such as silk spinning, masonry and carpentry.

TOP 10 TRADITIONAL CRAFTS

Embroidered tablecloths

1 Weaving
Traditional hand looms are still in use, made from cypress, walnut or mulberry wood by skilled craftspeople.

2 Embroidery
Rethymno was a major centre for embroidery, a skill introduced to Crete in the Byzantine era.

3 Spinning
Older village women still spin wool into yarn using a spindle and distaff, a skill that hasn't changed since the time of the Minoans.

4 Musical Instruments
Crete has a very strong tradition of making musical instruments (see pp56–7), and many places still make the lyra, a three-stringed lap-fiddle, and the laouto (mandolin).

5 Church Embroidery
Crete's Orthodox monks and nuns embellish sumptuous church vestments with gold, silver and silk stitching.

6 Wood Carving
Olive, cypress and mulberry yield a hard wood much loved by skilled Cretan carpenters.

7 Leatherwork
Everything from shepherds' boots and mule harnesses to satchels, handbags and sheepskin garments.

8 Silversmithing
Silver jewellery and religious objects such as icon frames and crucifixes.

9 Lace
Silk kopanelli lace is made by bobbin weaving, a skill revived in Gavalochori.

10 Antique Weapons
The Cretan pallikari (warrior-hero) loved highly decorated weapons. Authentic antique weapons are highly valued.

TOP 10 **Famous Cretans**

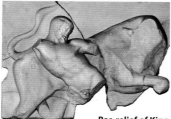

Bas-relief of King Minos with the Minotaur

5 El Greco

Born in the twilight years of Venetian rule in Crete, Domenikos Theotokopoulos (1541–1614) studied the icon painters of the Cretan School; their influence can be seen in the elongated features of his subjects and in his vivid use of colour. He trained under Titian in Italy, then moved to Spain, where he acquired his nickname, El Greco: "the Greek".

1 Zeus

Paramount among the Greek gods, Zeus was said to have been raised in caves *(see p54)*, sheltered from his child-devouring father, the Titan Kronos. Zeus later over-threw Kronos, giving rise to a new dynasty of gods.

2 King Minos

King of Crete, and both patron and tormentor of the ingenious Daedalus, Minos appears in the Greek myths as a tyrant. In fact, the legendary Minos is probably a composite of many Minoan kings.

6 Vitsentzos Kornaros

This poet (1553–1613), a contemporary of El Greco and Damaskinos, was a leading figure in the Cretan renaissance and is remembered for his life's work, *Erotokritos*, Greece's greatest post-Byzantine work of epic literature. Siteia Airport bears his name.

Effigy of Vitsentzos Kornaros

7 Nikos Kazantzakis

Born near Irakleio, Kazant-zakis (1883–1957) is best-known for his novel *Alexis Zorbas*, translated into English and filmed as *Zorba the Greek*. He was excommunicated by the Orthodox Church for his humanist views, and his self-penned epitaph reads: "I hope for nothing. I fear nothing. I am free."

3 George Psychoundakis

Born into a poor family in Rethymno, George served the resistance to the German occupation, both by acting as a mountain guide to British forces and as a message-runner between groups, as told in Patrick Leigh Fermor's translation of Psychoundakis' memoir *The Cretan Runner*.

4 Michael Damaskinos

Artist Michael Damaskinos (c.1530–92) is the best-known of the Cretan School icon painters. His works are traditional Byzantine in style but with Venetian influences. Some of his main pieces are in the Museum of Religious Art in Irakleio *(see p17)*.

Grave of Nikos Kazantzakis

Greek premier Eleftherios Venizelos

8 Eleftherios Venizelos

Born at Mournies, near Chania, Venizelos (1864–1936) made his reputation in the 1889 and 1897 uprisings. He led the campaign for union with Greece, and went on to become the Greek premier, dominating the nation's politics until the 1930s. Venizelos then became involved in a failed republican *coup d'etat* and was forced to flee the country, dying in exile in Paris.

9 Ioannis Daskalogiannis

Wealthy shipbuilder Ioannis Daskalogiannis (died 1771) raised the clans of the mountainous and inaccessible Sfakia region in the first major rebellion against the Ottomans in 1770. The uprising failed when Russian help did not materialize; Daskalogiannis surrendered at Frangokastello, from where he was taken to Irakleio to be tortured and skinned alive – not an uncommon penalty for rebels. Chania Airport was named after Daskalogiannis.

10 Chatzimichalis Dalianis

Dalianis, though a mainlander, ranks as an honorary Cretan for his local campaign during the Greek independence war. Ignoring local advice to wage guerrilla warfare like a Cretan, he and 385 followers chose in 1828 to occupy Frangokastello, where their enemies easily massacred them.

TOP 10 WORKS OF ART AND LITERATURE

1 *Zorba the Greek* by Kazantzakis
The freedom-loving spirit of Greece is to the fore in this tragi-comedy.

2 *Erotokritos* by Vitsentzos Kornaros
More than 10,000 lines of epic poetry written in the 15-syllable heptametric style, also sung as *mantinades* in Crete.

3 Paintings by El Greco
El Greco's only two paintings still in Crete are on display in Irakleio's Historical Museum *(see p17)*.

4 *Lord, Thou Art Great* by Ioannis Kornaros
This is one of Crete's most dazzling, intricate and famous icons; it resides at Moni Toplou *(see p45)*.

5 Paintings by Lefteris Kanakakis
Rethymno's Museum of Contemporary Art houses a variety of this artist's works *(see p48)*.

6 *The Bull from the Sea* by Mary Renault
A fictional retelling of the ancient myth of Theseus, Minos and the Minotaur.

7 The Cretan Journal of Edward Lear
Lear's illustrated diary of a journey to Crete in 1864.

8 *Officers and Gentlemen* by Evelyn Waugh
A pithy account of Commonwealth forces' retreat from Crete during World War II.

9 *Adoration of the Magi* by Michael Damaskinos
A portrayal of the veneration of the infant Jesus (Museum of Religious Art, Irakleio).

10 Frescoes of Moni Varsamonero
Later frescoes here, which span the period from 1360 to 1431, have been attributed to the 15th-century painter Konstantinos Rikos.

Kornaros's *Lord, Thou Art Great*

🔟 Myths and Legends

Medieval artwork showing an episode from the story of Theseus and Ariadne

① Theseus and Ariadne

After defeating the Athenians in war, Minos demanded tribute of youths and maidens to give to the Minotaur. Theseus, prince of Athens, slew the Minotaur and escaped the labyrinth with the help of Minos's daughter Ariadne, who gave him a ball of thread to retrace his steps.

② The Birth of Zeus

Zeus was the sixth child of the Titan Kronos, who had devoured his other children to prevent them from overthrowing him as he had overthrown his own father, Uranus, ruler of the old gods. Born in the Dikteon Cave in Crete, Zeus was hidden by his mother Rhea and raised in the Ideou Cave on Mount Idi. Zeus eventually poisoned Kronos, making him regurgitate his siblings, who overthrew the Titans to become the new gods and goddesses.

Vase portraying the death of Talos

③ Zeus and Europa

Though married to the goddess Hera, Zeus took many mortal lovers, one of whom was the princess Europa, daughter of the King of Phoenician Tyre. Taking the form of a white bull, Zeus carried Europa off to Crete, where he took her as his wife, siring three sons (including Minos).

④ The Immortal Plane Tree at Gortys

Zeus ravished Europa beneath this huge plane tree near the Roman ruins of Gortys. As a result, it is believed it never sheds its leaves, even in winter.

⑤ Talos the Bronze Giant

According to myth, Zeus created this bronze giant to defend Crete. Talos patrolled the coasts, hurling huge boulders to sink vessels that came too close. He was finally slain by Jason, with the aid of the sorceress Medea, who pointed out the giant's only weak spot, a vein near its ankle.

⑥ Nymphs of Dragolaki

The cave now known as the Dragolaki, or "Dragon's Lair", just outside the Sfakian mountain village of Agios Ioannis, is believed to be haunted by nereids, water-nymphs who were daughters of Nereus, a god of the sea.

7 Herakles and the Bull of Crete

The demigod Herakles, son of Zeus and the mortal woman Alcmene, was set 12 tasks by King Eurystheus, one of which was to capture and tame the untameable bull of Crete.

8 The Minotaur and the Labyrinth

In the myth of King Minos (one of the sons of Zeus and Europa), his queen Pasiphae bore a child, half bull and half man, after coupling with the sacred bull of Zeus. Minos imprisoned this monster, the Minotaur, in a subterranean labyrinth.

9 The Drosoulites of Frangokastello

Every May, phantoms are said to emerge from nearby sand dunes and ride into the Frangokastello fortress (see p46). They are the ghosts of Chatzimichalis Dalianis (see p53) and his men, massacred by Muslim Cretans here in 1828.

10 Daedalus and Icarus

Daedalus and his son, Icarus, made wings of feathers held together with beeswax to escape imprisonment at the hands of King Minos – their punishment for helping Theseus slay the Minotaur. Icarus flew too high, and the sun melted the wax, causing him to plummet into the sea, but Daedalus reached safety in Sicily.

Monument to Daedalus and Icarus, Agia Galini

TOP 10 CAVES

Inside the Dikteon Cave

1 Sfendoni
The most spectacular cave on Crete is crammed with strange rock formations deep beneath the Idi range.

2 Dikteon Cave (Diktaion Antron)
Said to be the birthplace of Zeus, this cave above the Lasithi Plateau contains an artificial lake.

3 Ideou Cave (Ideou Antron)
This enormous cavern on the slopes of Mount Idi was the childhood hideout of Zeus.

4 Kamares
This cave on Mount Idi's southern face lends its name to the sophisticated Minoan pottery discovered here.

5 Skotino
This is one of Crete's largest caves. It was first dedicated to the local virgin goddess Britomartis and later became a sanctuary to Artemis.

6 Inatos
The goddess Ilithia, daughter of Zeus and Hera, was worshipped in this grotto, which delves into the sea-cliff above Tsoutsouros.

7 Ilithia
Archaic stone figures of pregnant women have been found in this cave, birthplace of the goddess Ilithia.

8 Profitis Ilias
As with Diktaion Cave, this cave near Arkalochori also claims to be the cradle of Zeus.

9 Melidoni
This cave was said to be the lair of Talos, the bronze giant created by Zeus.

10 Cave of the Holy Fathers
This gloomy cave in the remote Selino highlands is now a Greek Orthodox shrine.

Music and Instruments

Traditional *askomandoura* player

1 Askomandoura (Bagpipe)

The *askomandoura*, or Cretan bagpipe, was once a popular instrument around the southern Aegean islands. Like some other seldom heard instruments, it is undergoing a minor revival as a new wave of younger musicians rediscover their musical roots.

2 Voulgari

The *voulgari*, a Cretan version of the long-necked lute known in Turkey as the *saz*, was a popular solo instrument in Cretan town music but is rarely heard now.

3 Santouri

The hammer dulcimer, or *santouri*, is an import from Asia Minor into Greece, where it was not widely played until the 1920s. The *santouri* probably evolved from harp-like instruments, such as the *lyra* of the ancient Cretans.

4 Gerakokoudouna (Hawk Bells)

Cretan *lyra* players sometimes attach tiny copper or silver hawk bells to the horsehair bows with which the *lyra* is played. These little bells are not just ornamental; they provide an occasional lively and rhythmic jingling accompaniment.

5 Kithara (Guitar)

The guitar, whether acoustic or electric, has sadly ousted many of the older instruments and, even at village festivals, weddings and saints days, has become a standard member of the Cretan ensemble.

6 Lyra

The three-stringed *lyra* is typical of Crete, although it is also found on several nearby islands. Distinctly pear shaped, it has a rounded body and short, stout neck with no frets. The *lyra* player props the instrument on one knee and plays it with a small bow, producing melodies that may be merry, martial or melancholy.

Musicians, including a *lyra* player

Daoulaki, Toumbi
There are two names for this drum particular to villages around Siteia. The Daoulaki is played with two sticks, and varies in size from 12 inches (1 foot) to 48 inches (4 feet) in diameter. It is now rarely seen or heard.

8 Laouto
The *laouto* is the Cretan version of the mandolin and is one of the most important instruments for Cretan musicians and composers. It is usually used to provide a backing rhythm for the *lyra*, and like the *lyra* is an essential member of any Cretan ensemble. However, the *laouto* is increasingly heard as a solo instrument.

Bouzoukis and other instruments

Bouzouki
This long-necked, fretted lute with four double strings is of Middle Eastern origin but has existed in Greece since the 19th century. *Bouzouki* music gained popularity in mainland Greece after the exchange of Greek and Turkish populations in the 1920s, but until after World War II it was heard less in Crete.

Baglamas
Not indigenous to Crete, this small stringed instrument was made by prisoners or the poor from a dried gourd, or sometimes a tortoiseshell, for a sound box and wire strings.

TOP 10 TRADITIONAL SONGS AND DANCES

Greek men dancing the *syrtos*

1 Syrtos
Performed all over Greece, the *syrtos* is undoubtedly the best-known of the Greek circle dances.

2 Pidiktos
The *pidiktos*, a dance from eastern Crete, involves great athletic leaps and bounds.

3 Pentozalis
The *pentozalis'* sprightly rhythms are reminiscent of the jigs and reels of Irish and Scottish folk music.

4 Sousta
A flirtatious couple's dance for the young, and a favourite at weddings and festivals.

5 Hasapikos ("Zorba's Dance")
The *hasapikos*, or "butcher's dance", provided inspiration for "Zorba's Dance" in the film *Zorba the Greek*.

6 Siganos
The dignified *siganos* dance is favoured by groups of men and women at festivals.

7 Mandinades
These traditional rhyming couplets, often satirical, are typical of Crete's rich oral tradition, with many improvised on the spot at festivals.

8 Rizitika
Stately elegies for historical events and personalities, with explicit or metaphorical lyrics, often performed as a capella, from Chania province.

9 Haniotis
The *haniotis* is a dignified line dance for men and women that originates from Chania.

10 Tabachaniotika
The Cretan, 1920s-30s version of the pan-Hellenic rembetika, songs of the urban underworld made popular by refugees from Asia Minor, some of whom settled on Crete.

Villages

Shops lining the streets of Kritsa village

1 Kritsa
MAP N5 ■ Lato 8am–3pm Tue–Sun

Sweeping views downhill and a reputation as one of the best craft centres of eastern Crete ensures that Kritsa sees its fair share of tourism. Its main street is packed with shops selling leather satchels and sandals, embroidery and brightly patterned rugs. About an hour's walk from Kritsa is the minor archaeological site of Lato, where you can see the remains of a Classical Greek city.

2 Argyroupoli
MAP E4

Western Crete's prettiest mountain village is tucked in the foothills of the Lefka Ori, on the site of the Hellenistic town of Lappa. The slopes of its valley setting flourish with lush greenery, watered by natural springs. Argyroupoli makes a good base for fairly easy walking in the surrounding hills.

3 Elos
MAP B3

Elos is one of the settlements known as the Enea Choria ("Nine Villages"), which are set among the chestnut forests of the Selloni region. At 600 m (1,970 ft) above sea level, it can be pleasantly cool in summer. Elos has a 14th-century Byzantine chapel and a ruined Ottoman aqueduct.

4 Alikianos
MAP C2

A ruined Venetian castle of the aristocratic Molini family *(see p46)* and a noted 14th-century church of Agios Ioannis (or "Ai-Kir Yanni" in local Cretan dialect) are the prime sights of Alikianos. The village is picturesque in itself, however, and is surrounded by citrus groves.

5 Kournas
MAP E3

Kournas nestles at the foot of Mount Dafnomadara, close to Crete's only freshwater lake. Its old stone houses cluster around a steep main street, and the village has two Byzantine-Venetian churches, dedicated to Agios Georgios and Agia Eirini.

6 Hamezi
MAP Q5

Above the Bay of Siteia, Hamezi has been inhabited since the Minoan era. Remnants of Minoan buildings can be seen on a hilltop from the present village, which is a peaceful cluster of whitewashed stone cottages, offset by colourful displays of flowers.

7 Ethia
MAP Q5

During Venetian occupation, this now desolate hamlet was the fief of the De Mezzo family. Their family manor has been admirably restored and has a small display on life in Venetian Crete.

8 Topolia
MAP B3

This village, en route from Kastelli to Paleochora, stands amid farm terraces, fields and olive groves, in a well watered valley which leads into Kartsomatados Gorge. Its small church of Agia Paraskevi dates from the late Byzantine era.

Stone church in the village of Axos

9 Axos
MAP H4

On the most direct route from Perama to Anogeia, off the old highway between Irakleio and Perama, Axos has striking views and an attractive Byzantine church dedicated to Agia Eirini. The village is a popular stop for excursion groups, and its tavernas and souvenir shops become crowded around lunchtime. On the hillside above Axos are a few scattered remnants of an ancient settlement.

10 Voila
MAP Q5

Voila is Crete's most dramatic ghost village, with lizards scuttling across its ruined walls and crumbling doorways. Voila is overlooked by the tumbledown walls of a Venetian hilltop castle and an Ottoman tower, and the only building still intact is the church of Agios Georgios. Surprisingly, two Ottoman-era drinking fountains still provide visitors with fresh water.

Aerial view of Lake Kournas

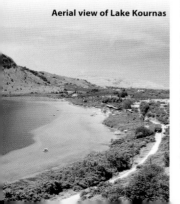

⭐🔟 Beach Resorts

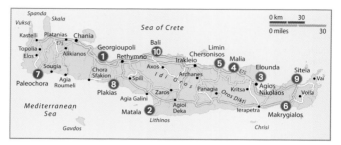

1 Georgioupoli
MAP E3

At the mouth of a pretty river, 20 km (12 miles) west of Rethymno, lies the quiet resort of Georgioupoli. The hub of the village is provided by a taverna-lined square shaded by eucalyptus trees. Georgioupoli's hotel and self-catering accommodation is spread out along a vast sandy beach.

2 Matala
MAP G6

Matala's coves of fine golden sand, surrounded by rocky red cliffs harbouring Roman cave-tombs, made the place a magnet for hippy travellers in the 1960s. Its tourism is more orthodox now, but Matala is still pleasantly low-key. A good base for exploring Gortys and Phaistos.

Artificial caves at Matala beach

Crystal-clear waters at Elounda

3 Elounda
MAP N4

Overlooking the turquoise waters of the Gulf of Mirabello and Spinalonga island, Elounda lies 11 km (7 miles) north of Agios Nikolaos, in eastern Crete. Formerly a peaceful fishing village, it is now one of Greece's most luxurious destinations, with the highest concentration of five-star resort hotels after Santorini.

4 Malia
MAP M4

With its great sandy beach and close proximity to Irakleio International Airport, Malia was destined to become one of the island's liveliest package holiday resorts. In July and August it is thronged, attracting a young crowd with its watersports and pulsing nightlife. There are peaceful spots to be found, too.

Limin Chersonisos
MAP M4

The biggest and busiest of the island's resorts, Limin Chersonisos straddles the north coast highway – a long double strip of hotels, bars, restaurants, dance clubs and shops. Catering mainly for package holiday-makers, it has now almost merged with the neighbouring resorts of Stalida and Malia.

Sheltered Souda beach, just west of Plakias

Makrygialos
MAP Q5

Makrygialos has the best beach in southeastern Crete, a swathe of grey sand and shingle beneath pine-covered slopes. This and its neighbour Analipsi have melded into a single chain of tavernas and guesthouses.

Paleochora
MAP B4

On a headland crowned by a dilapidated Venetian castle, Paleochora is part-fishing village, part-resort. It has a crescent of yellow sand on the west side of the promontory and a less crowded pebbly beach on the east.

Plakias
MAP F4

A huge sweep of clean grey sand attracts visitors to this small south-coast resort, but there are even better nearby beaches just west at Souda (backed by palm trees) and east around Damnoni, where there are three coves to choose from. Plakias is one of the island's quieter beach resorts, and its accommodation is mostly self-catering apartments.

Siteia
MAP Q4

The beach at Siteia stretches for miles east of the town and is backed by a ramshackle strip of hotels, guest-houses and cafés. This quiet port on Crete's northeast coast will become livelier once Siteia Airport begins receiving more international flights.

Bali
MAP H3

A small resort, purpose built around coves on the north coast, Bali comes to life in high season, when its "Paradise Beach" (officially Livadi) glistens with sunbathing bodies.

Holiday-makers on the beach at Bali

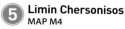

Areas of Natural Beauty

1 Imbros Gorge
MAP D4 ▪ 7am–sunset ▪ Adm charge in summer

The Imbros Gorge extends between the villages of Komitades and Imbros. Its narrowest point is 2 m (6 ft) wide. It takes 3 hours to walk through it.

Imbros Gorge's dramatic landscape

2 White Mountains (Lefka Ori)
MAP C–D4

The White Mountain region of Crete is one of Europe's pockets of wilderness, a region of savage, gaunt mountains traversed by deep gorges through which small streams flow in springtime. The best-known of these is the lovely Samaria Gorge (see pp30–31). In winter, the White Mountain peaks are covered with snow, but in summer temperatures can rise to more than 35° C (95° F).

3 Lake Votamos (Zaros)
MAP J5

Fed by an underground spring which provides Crete with most of its bottled mineral water, Lake Votamos is a deep-blue ring of cool, clear water surrounded by flinty, barren slopes. Tavernas near the shore serve grilled trout from the lake, and a good gorge walk starts nearby.

4 Aspros Potamos
MAP P5

The valley of the "white river" – which, like most Cretan watercourses, flows only in winter and spring – reaches the sea at the eastern end of Makrygialos beach. Surrounded by boulder-covered slopes, pines, terraced fields and olive groves, Aspros Potamos offers a pleasant walk with handsome Pefki village as the ideal start-point.

5 Omalos Plateau
MAP C3

A fertile plain ringed by rocky slopes, the plateau lies 1,050 m (3,445 ft) up on the northern side of the White Mountains. Millennia of winter rains have washed the topsoil down from the surrounding slopes to create this upland oasis. Most people tend to pass through without stopping, but, especially during spring, this is one of the prettiest, most peaceful spots in Crete.

Ruins on the islet of Elafonisi

 Lake Kournas
MAP E3

Terrapins and migrating water birds are among the wildlife to be spotted in and around Crete's main body of fresh water. The lake is prettiest in spring and early summer and is ideal for a swim.

Birds on the shores of Lake Kournas

 Vaï
MAP R4

A group of sturdy native Cretan palms on a crescent of sandy beach at Vaï is the largest of several such around Crete; others include Preveli and Souda, Plakias. The species is named after the ancient botanist who described it. Today the palm grove is carefully protected.

8 Kourtaliotiko Gorge
MAP F4

Frogs, terrapins, crabs and tiny water snakes splash and slither in freshwater pools at the bottom of the pretty canyon which emerges below Preveli on the south coast.

 Elafonisi
MAP A4

This tiny islet, a stone's throw from the mainland, may in the past have been a preserve for deer since its name means "deer island". Between Elafonisi and the shore is a lagoon of turquoise water. It is possible to reach the island simply by wading *(see also p84)*.

 Lasithi
MAP M4

Few of the thousands of white-sailed buildings in this "Plain of Windmills" still exist in working order. That said, the drive to this bowl of rich farmland surrounded by mountains is stunning in itself. Lasithi's patchwork of fertile fields, gardens and orchards strikes a contrast with the treeless grey slopes surrounding it.

Windmill on the Lasithi Plateau

Mountain Walks

Hiking through the Samaria Gorge

1 Samaria Gorge

Passing through the rugged scenery of the Samaria National Park, the Samaria Gorge is Crete's most popular walk. The track descends steeply at first from the Omalos plateau, then passes through pine woods, wildflower meadows and ruined villages to emerge at the small resort of Agia Roumeli *(see pp30–31)*.

2 Across the Lefka Ori
MAP C–D4 ■ Eos Mountain Refuge, Kallergi ■ 28210 44647 ■ Open Apr–Oct

A two-day traverse of the savage, treeless wilderness of the high White Mountains is spectacular, but only for very fit, experienced mountain walkers. The White Mountains rise to a 2,453 m (8,048 ft) peak, and walkers should note that it is bitterly cold in winter and scorchingly hot in summer.

3 Imbros Gorge
MAP D4

The gorge, which cuts through the eastern foothills of the White Mountains, is a slightly shorter hike than the better-known and much busier Samaria Gorge, but it is almost as spectacular and – especially in spring and autumn – allows you to escape from the crowds of day visitors.

4 Hochlakies Gorge
MAP R4

Beginning just outside Hochlakies village near Siteia, an easy, distinct path threads this gorge past striking rock formations. At the bottom, 45 minutes along, lies idyllic, sandy Karoumes beach. After a swim, walkers can retrace their steps.

5 Climbing Mount Idi
MAP H4

The ascent of 2,456 m (8,060 ft) Mount Idi, Crete's highest mountain, begins on the Nida Plateau. The trail (7–8 hours up and down) is best tackled on a long May or June day; expect snowdrifts near the summit chapel.

Trekking across the Lefka Ori

Kapetaniana, near Mount Kofinas

6 Mount Kofinas
MAP K6

Give yourself half a day to climb from the remote village of Kapetaniana to the summit of Mount Kofinas, 1,231 m (4,040 ft) and back. There are fine views of Mount Idi, the Dikti range and the south coast.

7 Sougia–Agia Roumeli
MAP C4

This two-day trek begins in the beach resort of Sougia, on the southwestern fringe of the White Mountains, and climbs first through fields and pastureland, then meadows of wild-flowers and pine woods, onto barren slopes high above the sea, before descending to Agia Roumeli. It is a difficult trek requiring astute navigational skills and a good map.

8 E4 European Long-Distance Path

Recommended only for very fit and experienced walkers, this is a long, arduous trek with variable route markings: yellow-and-black metal signs, poles or painted rocks. It is, effectively, a traverse of the entire island of Crete that takes at least 30 days to complete, from Kissamos in the west to Palaikastro in the east.

9 Zakros Gorge
MAP R5

The walk through the Zakros Gorge, also known as the "Valley of the Dead", snakes through a dramatic landscape, following a dry stream bed through eroded limestone cliffs with caves that were used as tombs by the Minoans. An aqueduct supplies potable water.

10 Agia Roumeli–Loutro
MAP C–D4

This one-day walk follows a path along the sand and pebble beach of Agios Pavlos, then climbs the steep Sellouda cobbled stair-path onto a high, pine-wooded plateau. It later descends into the Aradena Gorge, before zigzagging down a steep cliff to the delightful holiday village of Loutro.

The coastal village of Loutro

Top 10 Wildlife

A Cretan spiny mouse with her young

1 Cretan Spiny Mouse

The Cretan spiny mouse is unique to the island. Like most small rodents, it is nocturnal and is therefore not the easiest of the island's mammals to see. Look out for its endearingly large ears and blunt spines against rocky slopes at twilight.

2 Scops Owl

The tiny scops owl, with its grey plumage and bright yellow eyes, is common in Crete. This bird nests in holes in battered stone walls and roosts on roadside telephone poles or tree stumps. You are most likely to see scops owls at dusk, but after dark they can often be heard calling to each other – a monotonous, one-note hoot.

3 Scarce Swallowtail

Europe's largest butterfly is the dramatically patterned scarce swallowtail, its pale-yellow or white wings marked with dark zebra stripes and red and blue eye-spots. A strong flyer, this butterfly may be seen all over Crete in summer.

Scarce swallowtail

4 Gecko

Big-eyed gecko lizards, with sucker-tipped fingers that enable them to cling to walls and ceilings, inhabit many buildings, especially tourist lodgings around the island, coming out after dark to hunt insects. You may see several clinging to the wall near outdoor lamps, waiting to snap up moths and mosquitoes attracted by the light.

5 Lammergeier

The rare lammergeier vulture, Europe's largest bird of prey, may be seen soaring above the Omalos Plateau or in the high reaches of the White Mountains. Nicknamed the "bone-breaker", the lammergeier feeds on the carcasses of goats and sheep, and sometimes smashes bones open by dropping them from a great height to reach the marrow.

The majestic lammergeier vulture

6 Cretan Wild Cat

Cretan shepherds have long been claiming that the wilder parts of Mount Idi are home to a large wild cat known locally as the *fourogattos*. The first live specimen of this elusive beast was caught in the mid-1990s by Italian zoologists. Weighing 5.5 kg (12 lbs), with a tawny pelt and a formidable snarl, the Cretan wild cat is a rather startling re-discovery.

7 Pelican

The Dalmatian pelican, which breeds in the lakes and wetlands of northern Greece, Macedonia and Albania, migrates south to the Nile Delta for the winter. A few birds sometimes make landfall in Crete after being blown off course by storms, or by becoming exhausted by the force of strong headwinds.

Dalmatian pelican mid-flight

8 Cretan Argus Butterfly

This beautiful dark-brown butterfly is limited to the higher slopes of the Dikti and Idi mountains. It is increasingly endangered through loss of habitat.

9 Eleonora's Falcon

The very rare Eleonora's falcon breeds on some of Crete's offshore islands and can sometimes be seen performing its remarkable aero-batics above the steep cliffs of Zakros in eastern Crete.

10 Wild Goat

The Cretan wild goat, locally called *agrimi* or *kri-kri*, is one of Europe's rarest mammals. Perhaps 2,000 of these shy creatures live in the Samaria Gorge National Park, on the cliffs of the White Mountains and on Dia Islet off Crete's north coast.

A male Cretan wild goat

TOP 10 TREES AND FLOWERS

Cretan ebony on a mountainside

1 Juniper
Two species of this plant thrive on Crete: one stabilising sand dunes as salt- tolerant shrubs, the other inland as massive trees.

2 Cretan Ebony
Putting out spikes of pink flowers in spring, the Cretan ebony clings to steep, rocky cliffs and mountainsides.

3 Dragon Arum
With its foul-smelling red flower and spike, the dragon arum is a motif in several Minoan frescoes and a reality in shady spots beneath trees.

4 Yellow Bee Orchid
The yellow bee orchid, bearing flowers that imitate the insects it attracts, blooms on mountain slopes in spring.

5 Catchfly
With its ragged bright-pink flowers, the catchfly traps insects on the sap-coated hairs of its sticky stems.

6 Yellow Horned Poppy
This poppy lends a splash of colour to rocky stretches of the Cretan foreshore.

7 Giant Reed
The giant calamus reed grows as high as 4 m (13 ft) on the banks of streams.

8 Autumn Cyclamen
In October, flowering from apparently barren ground, the pink autumn cyclamen signals the end of summer.

9 Spring Crocus
This mauve flower with vivid yellow stamens flowers early in the year.

10 Evergreen Plane
Endemic to Crete, the tough evergreen plane has evolved to cope with the harsh environment. It is a subspecies of the common Oriental plane.

🔟 Nightlife

Dining al fresco in Paleochora

1 Paleochora
MAP B4

A hippy hideout well into the 1980s (see p102), Paleochora is still a laid-back spot. A handful of relaxed (and not too noisy) music bars are scattered along the Pebble Beach waterfront, and there are a couple of open-air clubs just outside the town.

2 Agios Nikolaos
MAP N4

Agios Nikolaos has a surprisingly lively after-dark scene compared with its day-time placidity. The town's nightlife hot spot is the pedestrianized Odos 25 Martiou (running uphill from the southwestern corner of the harbour), where there are half a dozen music bars, with as many again around the harbour. The town's club scene is more limited, with only one or two lively clubs (see also pp112–13).

3 Agia Pelagia
MAP K3

Lying 20 km (12 miles) west of Irakleio, this low-key resort is built into a steep hillside overlooking a sheltered bay, rimmed by a curving sandy beach. In summer, it is a popular after-dark escape for locals who come here for the waterside cocktail bars and seafood tavernas.

4 Platanias
MAP C2

Platanias is where most of Chania's younger residents go to party during summer weekends. There are at least a dozen great clubs, most with open-air dance floors. These clubs do not really start to get lively until well after midnight (see also p105).

5 Agia Galini
MAP G5

This small resort (see p93) has made catering to the party crowd its speciality. The cluster of bars and dance clubs around the harbour are buzzing by 11pm, allowing you to club-hop until the early hours.

The harbour of Agios Nikolaos at twilight

Busy taverna in Limin Chersonisos

 Limin Chersonisos
MAP M4

This former fishing village has become a continuous strip of bars, clubs, restaurants and guesthouses, stretching along some of the north coast's better beaches. Expect a multilingual (but mainly British) clientele (see p93).

7 Chania
MAP D2

Music blasts out from most of the cafés and bars along the harbourfront in Chania in the summer, and if you prefer an evening of bar-hopping and café-crawling to a night in the dance clubs, there are few better places in Crete. After midnight, younger Chaniots head to the clubs of Koum Kapi (east of the old walls) or Platanias (see also pp20–21).

8 Siteia
MAP Q4

The nightlife is less frenzied here than at other resorts along the north coast,

but a pleasant evening can be spent strolling from bar to bar along the quay. A few dance clubs also pulse behind the easterly beach road (see also p111).

 Irakleio
MAP K3

The nightlife scene in Crete's capital (see pp16–17) is more staid than in the resorts. Young locals congregate in the cafés and music bars located around Plateia Venizelou and Odos Chandakou.

 Rethymno
MAP F3

Most of the liveliest music-bars line Rethymno's old-town lanes inland from the harbour. Later on, the nightlife scene shifts to the open-air clubs in the resort area, along the seafront east of the centre (see also pp26–7).

Tavernas in the old town of Chania

🔟 Food and Drink

Classic *patsas* soup, made with tripe

1 Soup (Kreatosoupa and Patsas)

Cretan peasant cooking makes full use of any animal slaughtered. *Kreatosoupa* (meat soup) is made from the bones and left-over scraps of goat, mutton or beef, while *patsas* is a rich soup made with tripe. Both are often served at festivals, when a goat is traditionally slaughtered and spit-roasted for the guests.

2 Tsikoudia

Similar to Italian grappa, *Tsikoudia* or *raki* is a colourless spirit distilled from the skins and stems left after grape pressing. You may see market traders starting the day with a shot of *tsikoudia* and a strong coffee. It is also drunk after meals.

Tsikoudia, a traditional Cretan spirit

3 Cheeses (Staka and Myzithra)

Far more delicious than the ubiquitous feta are Crete's own cheeses. These delicious products include *myzithra*, which is made from fresh sheep's milk, and *staka*, which is made from whey.

4 Beer

Crete has two microbreweries well worth trying. Cretan in Chania makes three Charma labels (dunkel, lager and pale ale), while Brink's of Rethymno province is known for its organic dark and light beers.

5 Wines

Cretan wines are becoming more sophisticated as makers introduce techniques pioneered by New World producers. Most great wineries are in the Peza district of Irakleio province, but there are also some good wineries which can be visited near Siteia and Chania.

6 Cretan Sausages (Loukanika)

Loukanika – small spicy pork sausages – are found all over Greece, but those from Crete are reckoned to be among the best. The most famous ones hail from Sfakia district, and are served preferably grilled, though sometimes fried. They are a staple of *meze-dopoleia* (titbit eateries).

7 Greek Coffee (Kafes Ellinikos)

Finely ground robusta coffee beans and sugar are boiled together in small metal pots to make a thick, black drink, which is served up to customers in a tiny cup along with a tall glass of water. To order a sweet coffee, ask for *glyko*; for medium-sweet, ask for *metrio*; and for coffee without any sugar, order *sketo*.

Selection of fresh olives for sale

8 Olives

Crete and olives are basically inseparable. The olive has provided not only food, but also oil for lamps, and wood for fuel – without it, Crete might not have become the cradle of Minoan civilization. Olives are sold in a bewildering array of sizes and flavours, and Cretan olive oil (especially from Kolymvari district) is well-known overseas for its quality.

Snails with tomato sauce

9 Snails (Chochlioi)

Once a valuable source of protein, snails are now regarded as a delicacy. *Chochlioi* are either stewed in red sauce or sautéed *bourbouristi*-style with garlic, herbs and butter. Waiters give free extraction lessons.

10 Stamnagathi (Spiny Chicory)

Spiny chicory is the most esteemed of Crete's many wild greens, served lightly blanched. The picking season is early spring, but popularity ensures that it is grown throughout the year.

HERBS

1 Dittany
Taking its name from the Dikti mountains, this variety of oregano is unique to Crete and has long been credited with restorative powers.

2 Sage
Sage from the Cretan mountains is a favourite medicinal *tisane*, and is said to cure fever, chills, sore throats and rheumatism.

3 Saffron
Deriving from the crocus flower, costly saffron is used sparingly to add colour and flavour to soups and stews.

4 Fennel
Growing profusely in the countryside, this member of the carrot family has both edible shoots – ideal for stuffing fish – and a root used for cooking, particularly with cuttlefish.

5 Coriander
Coriander is used fresh as a flavouring and garnish for stews, grills and salads.

6 Cinnamon
Cretans acquired a taste for spices during the Ottoman and Venetian eras. Today, cinnamon flavours desserts like *ryzokalo* (rice pudding) and sweet pies.

7 Cumin
Another exotic import, cumin is essential in the slow cooked casserole dish, *stifado*.

8 Rosemary
Growing in abundance, rosemary is used by Cretans mainly to flavour fish dishes.

9 Mint
This ubiquitous wild herb scents the air on rural walks and flavours dozens of local dishes such as *keftedes* (meatballs).

10 Thyme
Sweet-scented thyme, with its deep purple flowers, grows wild on Crete's roadsides and hillsides.

A thyme bush in full bloom

TOP 10 Restaurants

The picturesque courtyard of Rethymno's Avli restaurant

1 Avli, Rethymno
This elegant courtyard restaurant is one of the best in Rethymno. Traditional grilled and roasted meat dishes are served alongside Cretan favourites such as *apatzia* (smoked sausages) and roast goat *(see p109)*.

2 Ta Dyo Rou, Rethymno
Traditional wine-and-food shop that serves dishes such as artichokes with broad beans, fennelled cuttlefish, or *stamnagathi*. The bread is good, and the wine commendable. It has ambient music *(see p109)*.

Outdoor tables at Tamam, Chania

3 Tamam, Chania
Popular with Chania's locals as well as with holiday-makers, Tamam has a menu that takes in cuisines from around the shores of the Eastern Mediterranean. Good choices for vegetarians, too *(see p109)*.

4 Balcony, Siteia
Run by a Cretan-French couple, Balcony offers Greek fusion cooking with Mexican, Asian and French influences. Wild herbs and local produce are extensively used in dishes ranging from traditional Cretan snails with tomato and goat's cheese to pork fillet with yogurt and pilaf rice *(see p119)*.

5 Portes, Chania
Presenting traditional Greek favourites with a modern twist, Portes stands out for its original cooking. Try the daily specials prepared with local ingredients *(see p109)*.

6 Methexis, Paleochora
On the east waterfront away from the main restaurant district, Methexis excels at keenly priced creative Cretan recipes cooked in limited quantities.

Try to arrive early to sit at a prime table. It is open all year round.

7 7 Thalases, Irakleio

Located east of the city centre in Nea Alikarnassos, close to the airport, 7 Thalases (which means "seven seas") is regarded by locals as one of Crete's best fish restaurants. Delights include squid with pesto, and sea bass with truffles and asparagus, plus a selection of exquisite sushi *(see p97).*

8 Poulis, Elounda

In a beautiful location on the waterfront, Poulis even has tables on a floating pontoon which, when lit up at night, make you feel like you are dining on a yacht. The fish, octopus and calamari are excellent, and the traditional meze are exceptional *(see p119).*

9 Veneto, Rethymno

The 14th-century vaults that house Veneto once contained a refectory for monks living in the cells above. Veneto's menu features a number of Cretan specialities, and the service is excellent *(see p109).*

Veneto restaurant's historic setting

10 The Ferryman, Elounda

With tables by the water's edge, this spot was named after the BBC serial *Who Pays the Ferryman*, which was filmed here. It serves Cretan specialities such as fresh lobster and roast mountain goat *(see p119).*

TOP 10 FISH SERVED IN CRETAN RESTAURANTS

Pan-fried *barbounia*, or red mullet

1 Fangri
Red porgy, prized for its delicate white flesh, is grilled and served whole; usually (but not always) one of the most expensive fish on the menu.

2 Melanouria
Saddled bream, common in spring, is variably sized, tasty and usually grilled.

3 Barbounia
Small red mullet appear on almost every tourist menu, pan-fried or grilled. Each fish provides only a few delicious mouthfuls – beware of bones!

4 Marides
Tiny picarel are dipped in flour and shallow-fried, then served with shredded lettuce and a slice of lemon.

5 Lavraki
Sea bass is baked in olive oil, red wine vinegar and rosemary, served whole.

6 Sardelles
Sardines are wrapped in vine leaves to seal in flavour and moisture, then grilled. Salted and pickled sardines are often served as meze.

7 Xifias
Swordfish keeps its flavour well when frozen, so it is a favourite with restaurateurs.

8 Skorpina
The evil-looking scorpion fish is surprisingly tasty and essential in Cretan fish soup; also served grilled.

9 Tonnos
Tuna steaks are best savoured in spring and autumn, when tuna migrate through Cretan waters.

10 Gopes
These nondescript, bony little fish are the cheapest on the menu, but delicious once the bones are removed.

🔟 Rural Tavernas

Colourful plate of typical Cretan food

1 Piperia, Pefki
MAP Q5 ▪ 28430 52471 ▪ €

Piperia serves traditional Cretan dishes prepared from seasonal and locally-sourced ingredients. Visitors can enjoy delicious food along with spectacular views of the coast and a laid-back atmosphere. On weekend nights, there may be live music and dancing.

2 Plateia, Myrthios
This village taverna attracts crowds for the views from its terrace over the Libyan Sea. Half of Crete seems to turn up on Sundays, but it is quieter during the week, with more time to enjoy the traditional cuisine and soak up the laid-back ambience (see p109).

3 Ta Douliana, Douliana
MAP E3 ▪ Centre of Douliana, on road between Kalyves and Vamos ▪ 28250 23380 ▪ Closed Mon ▪ €€

Situated in the centre of the tiny village of Douliana, this typical taverna's rickety wooden tables and chairs are set on a pretty terrace shaded by vines. The menu focuses on traditional, hearty fare such as *arni avgolemono* (lamb with lemon sauce). There is also a good selection of local cheeses and wines.

4 Goules, Goulediana
MAP F4 ▪ 10 km (6 miles) south of Rethymno ▪ 28310 41001 ▪ €

This traditional village taverna offers Cretan food with a twist. A highlight of the menu here is the roast pork in wine and honey sauce.

5 Palios Mylos, Argyroupoli
MAP E4 ▪ Piges Argyroupolis ▪ €

In Argyroupoli, known for its natural springs and cascades, Palios Mylos ("old mill") serves barbecued meat dishes, home-made cheese pies and salads at rustic wooden tables on a stone terrace shaded by plane trees.

6 Tou Zisis, Misiria
Zisis looks rather unprepossessing at first, housed in a drab concrete building. However inside, it serves some of the best food around – the grilled lamb alone is worth the short trip east of Rethymno (see p109).

7 El Greco, Lendas
El Greco has the day's dishes displayed in the kitchen for diners to choose from. Also on the menu are fish, octopus and grilled meats, served on a series of terraces above the beach. Book ahead (see p97).

Dining on the terrace at El Greco, Lendas

8 **Androulidakis, Gonia**
MAP F3 ■ 28310 31282 ■ €

Visit this family-run taverna for atmospheric alfresco summer dining. The extensive menu of Cretan favourites features dishes prepared with home-grown produce.

9 **Kalliotzina, Koutsouras**
An old-fashioned taverna with seaside tables, where visitors can venture into the kitchen to choose the ultra-traditional dishes of the day, or to perhaps watch a fish being grilled. Enjoy live Greek music twice a week (see p119).

Table with sea views at Kalliotzina

10 **Erotokritos, Ammoudara**
Popular with locals and tourists alike, Erotokritos is big, with an impressive stone dining room. It offers a vast menu with a huge range of delicious Greek starters (see p97).

TOP 10 CRETAN WINES

Wine cellar with various offerings

1 Domaine Fantaxometocho
Owned by Boutari, this Skalani village winery produces an excellent red from Kotsifali and Mandilaria grapes.

2 Domaine Paterianakis
This micro-winery makes an excellent rosé from Kotsifali and Syrah grapes.

3 Lyrarakis Legacy White
This 1966 winery has rescued near-extinct, local varieties by combining Vilana, Vidiano and Muscat Spina grapes.

4 Miliarakis Metikos
A rich, heavy red made from syrah and cabernet sauvignon grapes, best drunk with red meats and heavy sauces.

5 Sitia Cooperative Sitia White
A crisp, dry wine from blended Vilana and Thrapsathiri grapes, ideal for pairing with the local seafood.

6 Pnevmatikakis Kritopelagitis
From the up-and-coming Kissamos wine domain comes this dry white, blending indigenous Vilana and Romeiko grapes.

7 Economou Liatiko
Produced from vineyards on the very remote Ziros plateau in Crete's far southeast, this complex red shows a native grape at its best.

8 Miliarakis Estate PDP Red
One of the oldest Peza-region wineries produces this rich, oak-aged red from Kotsifali and Mandilaria grapes.

9 Gavalas An Rosé
Gavalas Winery prides itself on its organic production methods; this crisp rosé combines native Kotsifali with imported Cabernet Sauvignon grapes.

10 Lyrarakis Malvasia
Known in England as Malmsey, this dessert wine was exported everywhere by the Venetians. It is revived now in this blend of four white grapes, sun dried and oak-aged for a year.

🔟 Cafés and Mezedopoleia

Dining on meze at Ouzeri tou Terzaki, in the heart of Irakleio Old Town

① Avli tou Devkaliona, Irakleio

A night-time evergreen, right behind the Historical Museum, with courtyard seating beside a dry Venetian wall-fountain. Tuck into classic *raki* pairings such as *volvoi* (pickled hyacinth bulbs) or delicate *keftedakia* (mini-meatballs).

② Koukouvayia, Chania
MAP D2 ▪ Tafoi Venizelon

On a hillside close to the Venizelos family tombs, with sunset views over Chania, this café is much loved by locals for its home-made desserts – try the apple pie with cinnamon and whipped cream, or the rich chocolate mousse cake.

③ Avli, Agios Nikolaos
MAP N4 ▪ P Georgiou 12
▪ 28410 82479

This garden *mezedopoleio* is set in a courtyard shaded by grapevines and lemon trees. Delicious *mezedes*, as well as more elaborate dishes, are served with house wine made from their own vineyards in the Siteia hills.

④ Ouzeri tou Terzaki, Irakleio
MAP T1 ▪ Ioannou Marineli 17
▪ 28102 21444

A favourite among locals, Terzaki is one of a row of *mezedopoleia* on this narrow alley in the heart of Old Town. There are substantial meals on the menu; however, a drink and a selection of *mezedes* (such as the cheese-stuffed artichoke) is particularly recommended.

⑤ Kaaren's, Elounda

Check out this café's delicious breakfast, brunch, lunch and early evening cocktails for a welcome change from the regular taverna fare (see p118).

⑥ Kirkor, Irakleio

A classic bakery-café right by the Morosini fountain, Kirkor has tables spreading out into the square. The speciality is *bougatsa*, a flaky pastry available in either sweet-cream or salty-cheese versions.

Cheese pie, typical of Kirkor's menu

Offering a variety of coffees, it makes a perfect spot for breakfast, and it opens very early (see p96).

7 Apicorno Café, Kalyves
MAP D2 ■ Main Street

This modern café with large indoor and outdoor areas is open all day until late, throughout the year. It serves coffee, ice cream and drinks, plus breakfasts and snacks.

8 Mesostrati, Rethymno
MAP F3 ■ Kounoupa Lelas

Cretan specialities and drinks are served at this traditional café and meze bar. There are regular jam sessions in the evenings by acoustic musicians.

9 Rakadiko tou Andoni, Siteia

At a *Rakadiko*, drink (especially raki) is on a par with food. Eat as much as you like, either starters or mains.

Griechenland, Kreta, Ta Chalkina

10 Ta Halkina, Chania
MAP B5 ■ Akti Tombazi 29-30

This is one of the few old-port eateries favoured by locals. The highlight of Ta Halkina is the excellent Cretan cuisine and the live acoustic music played on most nights. The option of outdoor tables is available for those who find the music too loud.

TOP 10 MEZEDES DISHES

A plate of shrimp *saganaki*

1 Saganaki
Either a slab of fried or grilled cheese, or a cheese-based red sauce, studded with shrimps.

2 Marides
Tiny picarel are coated in flour, flash-fried and served with a slice of lemon and a dash of salt.

3 Loukanika
These smoked and spiced pork sausages are a typically Cretan snack, served more often in winter.

4 Baked Potatoes
Another typical winter snack served in mountain village *kafeneia*, often cooked in a wood-burning stove.

5 Octopus (Ochtapodi)
A favourite accompaniment to a glass of *ouzo*, *raki* or *tsikoudia* is a dish of octopus chunks cooked in oil, herbs and vinegar. Alternatively, try a grilled tentacle.

6 Kalitsounia
Small baked turnovers stuffed with crumbly soft cheese and herbs, sometimes drizzled with honey.

7 Askolymbroi
Boiled baby golden thistle – served root and sprout – has a brief fresh season; later in the year it's only available pickled.

8 Apaki
Smoked lean pork tenderloin, best made from young suckling pigs. Easy to make and serve, thus becoming ever more popular.

9 Omathies
A tasty rice and offal sausage, a local dish of eastern Crete.

10 Melitzanosalata
A savoury dip made by mashing grilled aubergines with garlic and chopped red pepper.

🔟 Markets and Shopping Streets

Shop in an archaeological museum

1 Museum Shops
MAP Q1

For quality replicas of finds from the archaeological sites of Crete, visit the Museum Shops in the former Venetian Loggia on Odos Paleologou in Rethymno, and in the Byzantine Museum in Chania.

2 Boutari Winery, Archanes
MAP K4 ■ 70100 Archanes ■ 28107 31617

The best wines from Crete (as well as from other parts of Greece) can be tasted and bought in this visitor centre at Crete's largest winery, built on the Fantaxometocho Estate outside Skalani village *(see also p91)*.

3 Odos Skrydlof, Chania
MAP B6

Running through the centre of the old quarter, this has been a street of saddlemakers and cobblers for centuries. These days, satchels, sandals and handbags abound.

4 Odos Daedalou, Irakleio
MAP T2

This pedestrianized lane is lined with fashion outlets and some major chains selling jewellery, and linen and cotton clothes to summer visitors.

5 Local Products Exhibition, Agricultural Co-operative Union of Siteia
MAP Q4 ■ Myssonos 74 ■ Open by appt: call 28430 29991

Promoting the produce of local farmers, this co-operative venture is well worth visiting just to see how the vines and olives of Crete are grown and processed. It is also a good place for quality olive oil, wine and *raki* – Crete's favourite spirit.

6 Chania Market, Odos Tsouderon, Chania
MAP B6

The market building is a Chania landmark and bustles with vendors and shoppers. A visual feast and also the place to buy herbs, olive oil, dried fruit, honey and typical Cretan souvenirs, such as *brikia*, the tiny metal pots used to brew Greek coffee.

Crowds browsing the stalls at the covered Chania Market

(7) Market next Municipal Gardens, Rethymno

MAP F3

An open-air market takes place in a car park here every Thursday from 7am until 1pm. Stalls sell local produce, fruit and vegetables, cheese, honey, flowers and clothing. There is also a smaller market on Saturday mornings in the square next to the bus station.

(8) Odos 1866, Irakleio

MAP T2–3

This is Irakleio's main market street and a great place to shop for Cretan herbs and herbal teas. It also offers an insight into the Cretan diet – along with the olives, you will see buckets of live snails for sale.

Coffee roaster on Irakleio's Odos 1866

(9) Odos Souliou, Rethymno

MAP Q1–2

Rethymno's upmarket shopping street is lined with stores selling copies of Minoan pottery, traditional Cretan pottery and modern ceramics, as well as colourful cotton and linen, lace and embroidery.

(10) Odos Ethnikis Andistasis, Rethymno

MAP Q2

The most photogenic market in Crete spills out – as it has for centuries – from open-fronted shops and stalls along Odos Ethnikis Andistasis and around the Venetian Porta Guora. Go early in the morning, when it is in full cry with waiters bustling from stall to stall with coffee and *raki*.

TOP 10 TRADITIONAL SHOPS

1 Komboloi 52, Chania
Dimotiki Agora Stall 52
Old-fashioned "worry beads" made from olive wood, amber, jet and turquoise.

2 Cretan Handicraft, Myrthios
74060 Myrthios
Vividly coloured weavings, embroidery, lace, herbs, wines, *raki* and olive oil.

3 O Armenis, Chania
Sifaka 14
This shop is the best surviving knife-dealer, fitting blades to personalized wood, bone or horn handles.

4 Voskakis Workshop, Amari Valley
Vizari Village
Nikos Voskakis hand-carves olive-wood platters, dishes, candlesticks and cutlery.

5 Nikos Siragas, Rethymno
Varda Kallergi 38, Old Town
Artistic wood-turner acquiring an international reputation for his beautiful handmade bowls, vases and works of art.

6 Vardaxis, Rethymno
Panou Koronaiou 31, Old Town
Superior ceramics, including plates, bowls, objets d'art and tiles of all sizes.

7 Ilias Maroulis and eta, Margarites Rethymnou
These two are among the best pottery shops in the area, with tastefully glazed practical ware, and more artistic pieces.

8 Tophanas, Chania
3 Angelou
Wonderful old Cretan rugs, saddle-bags and blankets.

9 Roka Carpets, Chania
Zampeliou 61
Naturally dyed, woven Cretan textiles.

10 Xylouris Popular Art, Anogeia
Mylopotamou
The ancient art of handloom weaving.

Woven items at Anogeia

Crete for Free

1 Kerasma

When you eat at a traditional Cretan taverna, you are often offered a *kerasma* (complimentary dessert) – generally *halva*, *kormos* (chocolate loaf), fresh fruit or yogurt with honey – as well as a glass of *raki* (a potent spirit) at the end of your meal. These are "on the house" – a symbol of Cretan hospitality. However, observance of this custom in upmarket or touristy tavernas is patchy.

2 Sunsets

Few experiences can beat watching the sun setting over the sea at the end of a hot summer day, either lying on the beach or sitting at a relaxed waterside café. As the afternoon heat subsides, the sky takes on orange, pink and purple hues. Pure romance.

3 Drinking Water

Tap water in Crete is good to drink – jugs of water are brought to tables, free of charge, at all bars, restaurants and cafés. Some visitors order bottled water, but this is not necessary. Good roadside fountains have queues of locals filling up.

4 Beaches

Beaches are free if you take your own towel and just lie on the sand – you pay only if you want to hire a sun bed and parasol. For pebble beaches, you might want to buy a roll-up reed beach mat to put under your towel.

Beaches such as Elafonisi are free

Rethymno's Archaeological Museum

5 Museums and Archaeological Sites

Most museums and archaeological sites offer free entry on 6 March (in memory of Melina Mercouri), 18 April (International Monuments Day), 18 May (International Museums Day), 28 October (Ohi Day) and on the first Sunday of each month (Nov–Mar).

6 Churches

Greek Orthodox churches have dark interiors, with candles and incense creating an eerily beautiful ambience. Look in during a service to hear the priest chanting religious texts. Both men and women should be dressed respectfully, with knees and shoulders covered.

7 August Full Moon

On the night of the August full moon, the Greek Ministry of Culture organizes free entry to all major archaeological sites, which stay open until midnight or 1am, and even stage performances in the grounds. On Crete, these sites include Phaistos, Gortys and Malia.

8 Hiking Trails

All hiking trails in Crete are free, except for the Samaria Gorge where you pay a small fee to enter Samaria National Park (this goes towards upkeep), and the Imbros Gorge. On some routes, you'll find wooden tables and benches where you can picnic, but bring water and sandwiches.

Hiking the Samaria Gorge in summer

9 European Music Day

www.europeanmusicday.gr

From 21–22 June each year (the summer solstice and the longest day of the year), European Music Day sees some free open-air concerts in various cities in Greece, including Chania and Agios Nikolaos on Crete.

10 Open-air Markets

All the larger towns host a street market, or *laïki agora*, with stalls stacked with colourful local seasonal fruit and vegetables, and cheap household goods. Crete supplies much of Greece with fresh produce.

TOP 10 BUDGET TIPS

Affordable dining at a taverna

1 Avoid peak season, which extends from early July to early September, when prices tend to rocket.

2 Look for cheap flights in May to June and September to October, when budget airlines are operating, but the island is wonderfully quiet.

3 Most museums and archaeological sites across the island offer cheap admission to children, students with ID and pensioners.

4 Some B&Bs and hotels offer decent discounts when you book a stay of a week or longer.

5 Eating out, you can make a meal of mezedes (starter platters), which are much cheaper and often more interesting than main courses.

6 Long-distance trekkers, especially following the E4, may camp for free in the high mountains and rural areas, without lighting open fires or littering.

7 Breakfast on *bougatsa*, a savoury-cheese or sweet-cream pie. Locals recommend Kirkor's *(see pp76–7)*.

8 Omnipresent *souvlaki* or kebabs make a tasty and nutritious takeaway meal in larger towns or resorts, and are cheaper than a sit-down dinner.

9 In tavernas, drink barrel wine served by the carafe, rather than expensive bottled wine.

10 Avoid point-to-point car hire on Crete, but return to the point of pickup. "One way hire" charges can be extortionate.

🔟 Festivals and Events

Greek Orthodox priests praying at an open-air Easter Mass

1 Epiphany
Islandwide ▪ 6 Jan

In the Greek calendar, Epiphany ends the 12-day reign of mischievous spirits who run loose during Christmas. Ceremonial rites banish the spirits until the next year, and baptismal fonts, springs and wells are blessed by priests. In all seaside locales, young men dive for the honour of recovering a crucifix tossed into the harbour.

Diving for the crucifix at Epiphany

2 Independence Day/Feast of the Annunciation
Islandwide ▪ 25 Mar

This national day commemorating the beginning of Greece's struggle for independence in 1821 is combined with the Feast of the Annunciation. There are religious processions and military parades, music and dancing.

3 Easter
Islandwide ▪ Mar–Apr

This is the Greek calendar's most important celebration. It is predominantly a family affair, focusing on the home, where spit-roasted goat or lamb is the highlight of a day of eating and drinking. Formal religious processions are led by elaborately-attired priests and are often followed by fireworks. In many towns and villages, Saturday night sees the shooting and burning of an effigy of Judas Iscariot.

4 St George's Day
MAP F3 ▪ Asi Gonia ▪ 23 Apr

Hundreds of shepherds bring their sheep anually to the church of St George in Asi Gonia village, near Rethymno. They seek their patron saint's blessings for a healthy flock and a prosperous season. In return the shepherds distribute free sheep's milk.

5 Mediterranean Festival
MAP Q4 ▪ Siteia ▪ End Jun/early Jul

Established in 2013, this is a big local world-music and jazz bash with three days and nights of free concerts and stalls selling handicrafts and local food. The venue is the Papies pedestrian zone on the waterfront.

6 Dormition of the Virgin Mary

Islandwide ■ 14 & 15 Aug

The Dormition of the Virgin Mary *(Kimisi tis Panayias)* is second only to Easter in importance, but it tends to be a much more public celebration. Church processions are followed by open-air eating and drinking in the churchyard or village square, which are followed by music and dancing until the early hours.

7 Festival of Agios Titos

MAP K3 ■ Irakleio ■ 25 Aug

The biggest celebration to mark the day of Crete's patron saint takes place at Irakleio, where icons and relics are carried through the streets of the city with great pomp. The saint's day is also celebrated with masses and other religious events at churches across the island.

8 Chestnut Festival

MAP B3 ■ Elos ■ Late Oct/ early Nov

This festival marking the chestnut harvest is enthusiastically celebrated in the village of Elos in southwest Crete. Music, dancing, drinking and eating chestnut-based dishes all play a part.

9 Arkadiou

MAP G4 ■ Moni Arkadiou ■ 7–9 Nov

Bust of Moni Arkadiou Abbot Gabriel

This patriotic three-day gathering commemorates the freedom fighters of the 1866 uprising and the defenders of Moni Arkadiou, who preferred to blow themselves up rather than surrender to the Muslim invaders *(see pp36–7)*.

10 Irakleio Summer Festival

MAP K3 ■ Irakleio ■ Early July to early Sept

Assorted concerts, plays and dance performances in various city venues, including old-town plazas and buildings.

TOP 10 SAINTS

Modern mosaic portraying St Paul

1 Agios Pavlos (St Paul)
The chapel of Agios Pavlos stands between Agia Roumeli and Loutro, though his biblical landfall was on the South Coast, at Kali Limenes.

2 Agios Nikolaos (St Nicholas)
The patron saint of seafarers and fishermen is honoured all around the coast of Crete.

3 Agios Titos (St Titus)
This follower of St Paul was ordained the first bishop of Crete.

4 O Taxiarchis Michael (St Michael)
The commander *(taxiarchis)* of the heavenly host is especially revered by combative Cretans.

5 Agios Georgios (St George)
St George is doubly popular as the patron of shepherds and a warrior saint.

6 Agios Efstathios
Efstathios (Stathis for short) is especially popular in southwest Crete, where many chapels and children bear his name.

7 Ag. Ioannis Theologos (St John the Divine)
St John wrote the *Book of Revelations* on Patmos, but he is also venerated on Crete.

8 Profitis Ilias (Prophet Elijah)
Many mountain-top chapels for this prophet may originally have been dedicated to the sun-god Helios.

9 Agioi Deka (Ten Saints)
Ten Cretan martyrs killed for their faith by the Romans have had a church near Gortys named after them.

10 Ag. Ioannis Prodromos (St John the Baptist)
St John is often shown in Orthodox art wearing a sheep-skin and having unruly hair, symbolizing his dwelling in the wilderness by the Jordan river.

Islands and Boat Trips

Hiking on Imeri Gramvousa island

Imeri Gramvousa
MAP B1

This pretty island crag just off the Gramvousa peninsula is crowned by a dramatic, crumbling castle. There are daily boat trips in season from Kissamos, and excursions through tour agencies in Chania.

2 Elafonisi
MAP A4

With its sandy beach and tropical blue lagoon, the tiny, low-lying island of Elafonisi is barely separated from the Crete shoreline. Daily boat trips from Paleochora (May–Sep) take an hour each way *(see also p63)*.

Elafonisi beach with its striking pink sand

3 Gavdos
MAP D6

Europe's southernmost point, where a few simple guesthouses, tavernas and beaches welcome visitors. Boats sail in summer from Agia Roumeli, Paleochora, Sougia and Chora Sfakion; the journey time is 3 to 4 hours. Check the timetable at www.anendyk.gr.

4 Paleochora–Agia Roumeli
MAP B–C4

The boat from Paleochora hugs the rugged south coast, calling in at the lazy resort of Sougia, before chugging along to Agia Roumeli, a cheerfully ramshackle village at the foot of the Samaria Gorge.

5 Agia Roumeli–Chora Sfakion
MAP C–D4

After marching up and down the Samaria Gorge, your journey can be extended along the coast by hopping on one of several daily boats that potter eastwards. All end up at the small port of Chora Sfakion.

6 Chrysi
The island of Chrysi ("Golden"), named for its sandy beaches, is known locally as Gaidouronisi ("Donkey Island") because of the Cretan habit of retiring elderly donkeys to uninhabited islands. Daily boat trips from Ierapetra take 45 minutes each way *(see p116)*.

7 Dia
MAP L3
A group of endangered Cretan wild goats have made their home on Dia. They can be visited on a day trip from Irakleio or Chersonisos.

8 Koufonisi
MAP Q6
Walking paths and beaches attract boats from Makrygialos, and a ruined Roman amphitheatre attests to a time when the island grew rich from the trade in murex, a sea mollusc from which imperial purple dye was made.

Sailing yachts anchored in Koufonisi

9 Spinalonga
The island of Spinalonga is completely covered by Venetian fortifications. Daily boat trips venture here in summer from Plaka, Elounda and Agios Nikolaos – a trip of five, 20 and 35 minutes respectively (see p111).

10 Andikythira
This makes an offbeat stop-off between Crete and mainland Greece to the northwest. From July to September, two weekly ferries sail from Kissamos to Andikythira, its larger neighbour Kythira and Gythio on the mainland.

TOP 10 WATERSPORTS

Windsurfing, a popular sport

1 Windsurfing
Boards are readily available for hire, and the best beaches are Georgioupoli, Chersonisos, Malia, Siteia and Plakias.

2 Snorkelling
Crete's crystal waters, teeming with colourful fish, are ideal for snorkelling.

3 Banana Rides
Inflatable bananas, towed at high speed and carrying up to half a dozen riders, are popular in Malia and Chersonisos.

4 Sea Biscuit Rides
Similarly popular is the "sea biscuit", a tough inflatable ring for a single rider.

5 Catamaran Sailing
Catamarans can be hired by the hour or day at most resorts, with instruction available for novice sailors.

6 Yacht Sailing
Yachts can be chartered "bareboat" (without skipper or crew), fully crewed or with a skipper only.

7 Scuba Diving
Although archaeological sites and ancient shipwrecks are off-limits, there are good dives to several wrecks from World War II.

8 Waterskiing
Waterskiing, though expensive, is available at most of the bigger resorts.

9 Waterparks
Near Chersonisos, Acqua Plus is a playground of waterslides, waves and waterfalls. There are smaller water-parks near Irakleio (Water City) and Chania (Limnoupolis).

10 Jet Skiing
Despite the introduction of rules limiting their use, jet skis can still be rented at all major resorts.

Crete Area by Area

Whitewashed houses lining the
sheltered harbour at Loutro

🔟 Central Crete

The landscapes of central Crete include beaches, rolling farmland and rugged mountains – among them, Crete's highest summit, Mount Idi, or Psiloritis. This was the heartland of Minoan civilization, and the most important Minoan ruins lie just south of the island's modern capital, Irakleio. Along the north coast are some busy resorts, while on the south coast, there are quieter places to enjoy a beach holiday.

Boats at the harbour of Irakleio

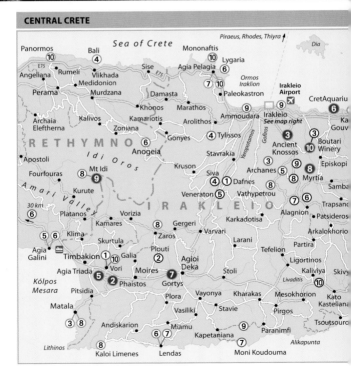

CENTRAL CRETE

1 Irakleio

The modern capital of Crete was badly damaged during World War II, and only a few of its old Venetian buildings survived the reconstruction of the city. However, its Venetian fortress, harbour, arsenal and city walls are still impressive sights. The city's main and most popular attraction is the fascinating Irakleio Archaeological Museum *(see pp18–19)*.

2 Phaistos

This labyrinth of ruins dating from around 1600 BC includes a Minoan courtyard and theatre with tiers of stone seats, a monumental stairway, peristyle hall and a vast central courtyard. The still undeci-phered Phaistos Disc, which was discovered here, is on display in the Irakleio Archaeological Museum

Ruins at the ancient site of Phaistos

(see p19). Phaistos was destroyed around 1450 BC by the cataclysms that also laid low Crete's other Minoan palaces. Not usually as crowded as the more famous Knossos, the site at Phaistos has an impressive location on a hillside above fertile farmland *(see pp24–5)*.

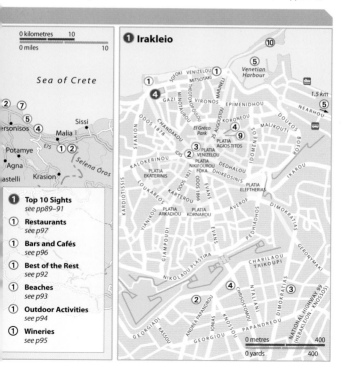

1 Top 10 Sights
see pp89–91

1 Restaurants
see p97

1 Bars and Cafés
see p96

1 Best of the Rest
see p92

1 Beaches
see p93

1 Outdoor Activities
see p94

1 Wineries
see p95

Vivid fresco in the palace of Knossos

3 Ancient Knossos

Knossos was pinpointed as an important archaeological site by the great Heinrich Schliemann, and unearthed by British archaeologist Sir Arthur Evans, starting in 1900. The columns, courtyards and coloured frescoes of this ancient Minoan palace still have the power to amaze. Knossos was lost to history after the cataclysmic volcanic eruption that hastened the decline of Minoan civilization, but the site is now one of the island's most impressive relics of the vanished world of the Minoans (see pp12–15).

4 Historical Museum of Crete

MAP S1 ▪ Sofokli Venizelou 27, Irakleio ▪ Apr–Oct: 9am–5pm Mon–Sat; Nov–Mar: 9am–3:30pm Mon–Sat ▪ Adm ▪ www.historical-museum.gr

Spanning the centuries from the Byzantine period right up to World War II, exhibits at this fascinating museum in Irakleio include Venetian monuments, Orthodox church frescoes, traditional folk costumes and two paintings by El Greco.

5 Agia Triada

MAP H5 ▪ 3 km (2 miles) W of Phaistos ▪ 28920 91564 ▪ 9am–4:45pm daily ▪ Adm; also combined ticket with Phaistos

Excavated in the early 1900s, Agia Triada is smaller than other Minoan sites such as Knossos and Phaistos, and was probably an aristocratic villa or a royal summer palace. Fine Minoan pottery discovered here, including three carved stone vases, is displayed in the Irakleio Archaeological Museum. Agia Triada draws fewer visitors than the larger sites, so you can explore its honeycomb of stone corridors, stairs and courtyards at your own pace.

6 CretAquarium

MAP K3 ▪ Irakleio ▪ 9:30am–5pm daily (May–Sep: to 9pm) ▪ Adm ▪ www.cretaquarium.gr

Situated just a 10-minute drive from Irakleio airport, this modern aquarium is home to around 2,500 sea creatures representing 200 Mediterranean species.

Sea turtle at CretAquarium

7 Gortys

Roman columns, a ruined Byzantine basilica, fortifications and remains of temples all hint at the past glories of this little-visited site. First settled in Minoan times, Gortys became one of the main cities of Doric Crete. Later a Roman provincial capital, it was one of Crete's most prosperous cities until it was sacked by Arab invaders in the 8th century AD (see pp28–9).

THE KNOSSOS ENIGMA

Most archaeologists believe that the maze of ruins at Knossos was a royal palace, the bustling hub of the greatest empire that the islands of the Aegean had ever seen. But a few "heretical" archaeologists claim that Knossos may actually have been a giant necropolis where kings and nobles were interred, as in the tombs of ancient Egypt.

8 Kazantzakis Museum

MAP L4 ■ Myrtia village square
■ 28107 41689 ■ Apr–Oct: 9am–5pm
daily; Nov–Mar: 10am–3pm Sun
■ Adm ■ www.kazantzaki.gr

Cretan author Nikos Kazantzakis
(1883–1957) is best-known for his
novel *Alexis Zorbas*, which was filmed
in 1964 as *Zorba the Greek*, starring
Anthony Quinn in the title role. The
author was born in Myrtia, and a
small museum in the Kazantzakis
family home is crammed with his
manuscripts and diaries, photos
and other memorabilia.

Display at the Kazantzakis Museum

9 Mount Idi

MAP H4

At 2,456 m (8,060 ft), Mount Idi,
which is also known as Mount Ida
and Mount Psiloritis, is Crete's
highest mountain. From the car-
accessible Nida Plateau, any fit and
properly shod mountain walker can
undertake the path climb up (allow
7–8 hours including the return trip).

10 Boutari Winery and Audio-Visual Show

MAP K4 ■ 2810 731617 ■ 9am–5pm
Mon–Fri, by appt on weekends
(Nov–Mar: 8:30am–4:30pm) ■ Adm

At the Fantaxometocho Estate, near
Archanes village, one of Greece's
leading winemakers has opened a
state-of-the-art audiovisual show
celebrating the island's landscapes,
history and way of life. The show also
highlights the vineyards and grape
varieties that produce some of the
Boutari family's award-winning wines.
You can sample and buy Boutari red
and white wines at the winery shop.

A MORNING IN IRAKLEIO

Start at the ornate **Porta
Kenouria** archway, once the main
entrance into the walled city –
Irakleio was fortified by the
Venetians to defend it against the
Ottoman Turks. Walk through the
gate and down Evans Street to
arrive on **Platia Kornarou**, with its
central six-sided stone building,
originally a pumphouse, now a
café. Next to it, the **Venetian
Bembo Fountain** incorporates
a headless marble torso from a
Roman statue.

Proceed north of the fountain,
along **Odos 1866** *(see p79)*, which
hosts Irakleio's daily market, with
stalls selling fresh fruit, olives
and nuts. Cross over Plateia
Nikiforou Foka to Plateia Venizelou, lined with cafés and centred
on the 17th-century **Morosini
Fountain** *(see p16)*, with four lions
holding up the main basin. Leave
the square by 25 Avgoustou
Street, pass the imposing Loggia
(Venetian Town Hall), then turn
immediately right to find **Agios
Titos** (St Titus) *(see p17)*. Originally
Byzantine, this church was rebuilt
by the Venetians, turned into a
mosque by the Ottomans and
later reclaimed by the Orthodox
Church in 1925. A reliquary
contains the skull of St Titus.

Continue down 25 Augoustou
to the seafront, then walk along
the causeway to the **Venetian
Fortress** *(see p16)*. Having
explored the old town, either
follow the seafront promenade
west to the **Historical Museum**
or visit the excellent **Irakleio
Archaeological Museum** *(see
pp18–19)* on the east side of town.

See map on pp88–9

Best of the Rest

1 Museum of Cretan Ethnology, Vori

MAP H5

One of the first museums to celebrate the lives of ordinary Cretans (see p51).

2 Palace of Malia

MAP M4

Only 3 km (2 miles) east of the bustling resort of modern Malia, this ruined Minoan palace once yielded fantastic treasures (see p42).

Remains of the Palace of Malia

3 Mount Giouchtas

MAP K4

To the south of Archanes, Mount Giouchtas is the mythical burial place of the god Zeus. The remains of a Minoan sanctuary are below the summit. Inhabited by eagles, vultures and other raptors, this has been declared a conservation area.

4 Minoan Villa Site, Tylissos

MAP J4 ▪ 28102 26470 ▪ 8:30am–2:45pm Tue–Sun ▪ Adm

Tylissos was inhabited more than 4,000 years ago, but the most interesting discoveries are the remains of three large Minoan villas.

5 Archanes Archaeological Museum

MAP K4 ▪ 28107 52712 ▪ 8am–3pm Wed–Mon ▪ Adm

The small farming town of Archanes has a surprisingly good museum with finds from nearby sites, which include clay Minoan coffins, fragments of pottery, and a ceremonial dagger that may have been used in human sacrifice.

6 Church of Archangelos Michail, Asomatos

MAP K4

The Archangel Michael, leader of the heavenly host, is known in Greek as "O Taxiarchis" (the Brigadier) and is depicted in armour, sword in hand, along with other saints in the frescoes within this pretty 14th-century church at Asomatos.

7 Koudouma Monastery

MAP K6 ▪ Dawn to dusk daily ▪ Donations welcome

The monks of Koudouma live in enviable isolation in a small monastery on a pebble beach, a long dirt-track drive down from Sternes village.

8 Vathypetro Minoan Villa

MAP K4 ▪ 28102 26470 ▪ 8:30am– 3pm Tue–Sun

Vathypetro was presumably the home of a Minoan landowner, and ancient wine-making equipment found on the site indicates that the surrounding vineyards are thousands of years old.

9 Mount Kofinas

MAP K6

A mere hillock by Cretan standards, but still a satisfying climb (starting from Kapetaniana village) with great views of Mount Idi (see p65) and the south coast.

10 Venetian Fortress, Irakleio

MAP U1 ▪ Old Harbour ▪ Adm

Known to the locals as the Koules, this sturdy 16th-century fortress was built by the Venetians to protect Irakleio's harbour. It reopened in 2016 following restoration. The rooftop offers impressive views of the town (see also p16).

See map on pp88–9

Beaches

 Malia
MAP M4

A long strip of bars, clubs, shops, hotels and apartments lines the main coast highway at Malia. The splendid sandy beach is crowded with sun loungers and umbrellas from early summer until September.

 Chersonisos
MAP M3

A big, brash resort that may soon grow to merge with neighbouring Stalida and Malia. The east beach is unarguably superb, and it has an excellent array of multinational bars and restaurants.

 Matala
MAP G6

A series of sandy coves separated by rocky headlands, Matala first attracted sun-seeking hippy travellers in the 1960s, including Joni Mitchell who wrote the song *Carey* here. It soon graduated to become a small holiday resort in the 1980s.

4 **Bali**
MAP H3

A small, purpose-built resort set around three coves sheltered by cliffs.

 Agia Galini
MAP G5

On a crescent bay where a reed-lined river meets the sea, this is a classic fishing village turned seaside resort. A day-trip will be needed to reach the beach.

6 **Dytikos (Lendas)**
MAP J6

One of the longest beaches on the south central coast, Dytikos is popular with naturists.

 Kato Gouves
MAP L3

With its long stretch of sand and shingle and growing number of package holiday hotels, this is one of the better beaches close to Irakleio.

 Kaloi Limenes
MAP H6

A relatively remote and peaceful series of small beaches and coves among dramatic cliffs. However, the offshore oil tanker terminal rather mars the view.

9 **Irakleio**
MAP K3

If you have time to kill while in the capital, head for the municipal beach at Amnisos, which is open from 9am to 7pm for a small fee.

 Panormos
MAP G3

One of the less developed beaches on Crete's central north coast, Panormos has a small stretch of sandy beach beside a miniature fishing harbour and a handful of places to eat and drink.

Swimmers in the turquoise waters near Agia Galini

Outdoor Activities

Visitors inside the Dikteon Cave

1 Hiking Crete
MAP M4 ■ Malia
■ www.hiking-crete.com

These half-day hiking tours whisk you into Crete's remote interior to explore the Roza Gorge, the Katharo Plateau or the Minoan Path, which ends at the Dikteon Cave.

2 Cycling Creta
MAP M4 ■ Analipsi, Chersonisos ■ www.cyclingcreta.gr

This company offers informative guided mountain-bike tours at various levels of difficulty. They cater for small groups and also offer free pick-up and drop-off from Irakleio, Gouves, Stalida and Chersonisos.

3 Enjoy Crete
MAP K3 ■ Irakleio
■ www.enjoy-crete.com

Sea-kayaking day and multi-day trips are arranged in either single or double kayaks, with instruction. The company also offers hiking tours for all ability levels.

4 Scubakreta
MAP M3 ■ Chersonisos
■ www.scubakreta.gr

This is a well-equipped scuba diving outfit offering courses (PADI) and organized boat and shore dives from its centre in Chersonisos.

5 Sailing Trips Crete
MAP T1 ■ Venetian Harbour, Irakleio ■ www.sailingtrips.gr

Take a half-day trip aboard a sleek sailing boat (maximum 8 persons). Tours depart twice daily from Irakleio to the islet of Dia *(see p85)*, with time for snorkelling, fishing and lunch.

6 Eurodiving
MAP K3 ■ Lygaria beach, Agia Pelagia ■ www.eurodiving.net

Scuba diving courses (PADI) for all levels, diving excursions and equipment for hire are all available here. Some 25 nearby dive sites include underwater caves and reefs.

7 Heraklion Diving Centre
MAP K3/L3 ■ Efodou 25, Irakleio/Chersonisos ■ www.heraklion-diving.com

Passionate, well established (since 1977), and professional diving instructors offer lessons at all levels, plus guided scuba-diving trips. Main sites, including a crashed German plane and Amphora Reef, are near Chersonisos.

8 Green Tour
MAP H4 ■ www.greentour.gr

A one-day guided hike up Mount Idi *(see p91)*, called "Crete from Above", is one of two day-long itineraries offered by this Rethymno-based company. The trip includes lunch at a shepherd's hut.

9 The Hub MTB Adventures
MAP M4 ■ Malia ■ www.mtbhub.gr

Taking you away from the crowds, into rural Crete, these mountain-bike excursions cover nearly a dozen off-road itineraries of all difficulties, including single-track.

10 Stay Wet Diving
MAP K3 ■ Mononaftis beach, Agia Pelagia ■ www.staywet.gr

A major advantage of this PADI-affiliated operator, especially for those who hate long boat rides, is the ability to dive straight off the beach.

Wineries

1 Douloufakis
MAP J4 ◼ Dafnes, 18 km (11 miles) S of Irakleio ◼ www.cretanwines.gr

Set amid lush vineyards and olive groves, Douloufakis was founded in 1930. Welcoming and knowledge-able, it runs tours and tastings of its award-winning wines.

2 Zacharioudakis
MAP J5 ◼ Plouti, 48 km (30 miles) SW of Irakleio ◼ www.zacharioudakis.com

Near Gortys and the south coast, this modern, purpose-built hillside winery produces organic wines and is open for tours and tastings.

The wine-tasting facilities at Boutari

3 Boutari
The tour at Boutari (see p91) takes you through its vineyards, production area and cellars. Visitors then watch a short film about wine-making, followed by a tasting.

4 Daskalakis
MAP J4 ◼ Siva Palianis, 17 km (10 miles) S of Irakleio ◼ www.silvawines.gr

Located near Dafnes, this family-run business dates from 1890. All its wines are certified organic, and its Sauvignon Blanc is outstanding. Open for tours and tastings.

5 Idaia
MAP J4 ◼ Veneraton, 18 km (11 miles) S of Irakleio ◼ www.idaiawine.gr

This winery focuses on quality rather than quantity. Sample Idaia's award-winning velvety red Ocean, its extra-dry single varietal Vidiano white or its Grenache Rouge rosé.

6 Lyrarakis
MAP L4 ◼ Alagni, 18 km (11 miles) S of Irakleio ◼ www.lyrarakis.com

Credited with reviving the two ancient local varieties, Daphni and Plyto, this winery dates from 1966 and offers informative tours and tastings with savoury snacks.

7 Paterianakis
MAP L4 ◼ Alagni, 18 km (11 miles) S of Irakleio ◼ www.paterianakis.gr

With a hilltop tasting room that affords spectacular views over the surrounding vineyards, this welcoming winery prides itself on an all-organic product line.

8 Minos Miliarakis
MAP L4 ◼ Peza, 17 km (10.5 miles) S of Irakleio ◼ www.minoswines.gr

Trading in its present form since 1932, this high-capacity winery makes wine from a wide variety of indigenous and imported grapes. Visits take in a small museum as well as tasting facilities.

9 Stilianou
MAP L4 ◼ Kounavi, 12 km (7 miles) S of Irakleio ◼ www.stilianouwines.gr

The mountain vineyards of this boutique winery produce limited quantities of organic wines, sold in numbered bottles. Stilianou is open all year for tastings.

10 Strataridakis
MAP L5 ◼ Arkalochori, 33 km (20 miles) SE of Irakleio ◼ www.strataridakis.gr

Now run by two brothers, this winery dates from 1955. Just a limited number of wines (8 labels) are currently produced.

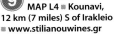

See map on pp88–9

Bars and Cafés

Outdoor tables and a fountain outside Irakleio's Mare Café

 Mare, Irakleio
MAP S1 ■ Sofokli Venizelou
■ 2810 41946

Located on the waterfront, Mare serves coffee and light snacks by day and cocktails by night. Enjoy the sunset on the café's lovely terrace.

2 The Bitters Bar, Irakleio
MAP T2 ■ Stoa Platia
Liontarion 25

In a covered arcade close to the Morosini Fountain, this bar serves morning coffee, plus an extensive range of expertly shaken cocktails.

3 Kirkor, Irakleio
MAP T1 ■ Liontara Square

Start the day with a Cretan-style breakfast of coffee and a cream-filled *bougasta* while enjoying the view of the Lion Fountain *(see pp76–7)*.

4 Pagopoieion, Irakleio
MAP T2 ■ Platia Agios Titos
■ 2810 221294

This bistro bar is installed in an old ice factory. It occasionally hosts musical performances in the wonderful space upstairs *(see p76)*.

 New York, Chersonisos
MAP M3 ■ 28970 23415

Enjoy breakfast, snacks and cold drinks during the day at this beach bar by the harbour entrance, and party to the lively music at night.

6 C'est La Vie Bar, Agia Galini
MAP G5 ■ In the harbour ■ 28320 91113

Enjoy breakfast, crêpes, coffee, drinks and ice cream at this bar with a view of the harbour.

 **Almyra Seaside, Agia Pelagia**
MAP K3 ■ On the beach

With sun beds and parasols for hire, this slick beach bar and restaurant serves creative Mediterranean fare and cocktails on a terrace shaded by tamarisk trees, overlooking the bay.

8 Port Side, Matala
MAP G6 ■ Above the beach
■ 694 5983 886

A café-bar right above the beach, Port Side serves snacks and drinks (alcoholic and soft) and often has a DJ event on Friday evenings.

 Dish Bar, Irakleio
MAP T2 ■ Papagiamali 3

In a Neo-Classical building by Agios Titos, this bar-restaurant offers food, drinks and music till the early hours.

10 Nefeli, Agia Pelagia
MAP K3

Friendly service and a welcoming vibe make this lounge bar popular with holiday-makers. Known for its good coffees – usually hard to find on Crete – and well-mixed cocktails.

Restaurants

PRICE CATEGORIES

For a three-course meal for one with half a bottle of wine (or equivalent meal), taxes and extra charges.

€ under €25   €€ €25–40   €€€ over €40

Ippokambos, Irakleio
MAP S1 ■ Sofokli Venizelou 3 ■ €

On a terrace overlooking Irakleio's seafront promenade, this informal eatery serves simple seafood dishes. Order grilled sardines, fried squid, a salad and a carafe of white wine – all tasty and reasonably priced, hence the queues.

② Erganos, Irakleio
Georgiadou 5 ■ 2810 285629 ■ €

Savour traditional Cretan cooking in an appropriately folksy environment. Signature dishes include snails, lamb's liver, or sweetbreads and grilled mushrooms.

③ Kyriakos, Irakleio
Leoforos Dimokratias 53
■ 2810 222464 ■ €

In traditional taverna style, you will be beckoned into the kitchen at this old-fashioned restaurant with smoke-stained, wood-panelled walls. Choose your meal from bubbling pots or glass cases filled with fish, chops and vegetables.

④ Kipos Ton Gefseon, Irakleio
MAP T3 ■ Chrisostomou Av. 8
■ 2810 300358 ■ €€

Housed in a stylish old villa, this restaurant offers traditional Cretan food. You can eat indoors or in the lovely garden surrounded by trees.

⑤ 7 Thalases, Irakleio
MAP K3 ■ Irakleitou & Irodotou 1, Nea Alikarnassos ■ 2810 342945 ■ €€

This welcoming eatery specializes in local seafood. Dine here on fresh fish, salad and a bottle of white wine. It lies east of town, near the airport.

⑥ Aetos, Anogeia
MAP H4 ■ Upper village
■ 28340 31262 ■ €

A traditional village taverna, Aetos specializes in lamb and goat cooked on a wood-fired grill. It also serves a variety of excellent local cheeses.

⑦ El Greco, Lendas
MAP J6 ■ Above the beach
■ 28920 95322 ■ €€

Overlooking the Libyan Sea, El Greco offers traditional food made with local ingredients, plus an extensive wine list. Reservations required *(see p74)*.

⑧ Elia, Zaros
MAP J5 ■ 1.5 km (1 mile) outside Zaros village ■ €€

Elia is the restaurant of the Eleonas Country Inn. All the standard dishes are served inside or outside, in a rustic wood-and-stone environment.

Charming dining terrace at Elia

⑨ Erotokritos, Ammoudara
MAP K3 ■ Papandreou 109
■ 28102 52426 ■ Noon–midnight ■ €

This taverna serves traditional Cretan fare. Its white wine from the barrel is particularly good *(see p75)*.

⑩ Alekos, Vori
MAP H5 ■ By Agia Pelagia church ■ 28920 91094

Lovely courtyard-house taverna with food to match, offering large portions. Chef-owner Alekos has spent time in Belgium, which is reflected in his style of cooking.

See map on pp88–9

ⓂⓄ Western Crete

Rethymno's fortress

Much of western Crete is dominated by the jagged peaks of the Lefka Ori (White Mountains), which are often snowcapped until June. Traversed by spectacular gorges, the mountains drop sharply to the Libyan Sea on Crete's south coast. These mountains were for centuries the heartland of islanders' resistance to foreign occupiers. Many of the remoter villages were accessible only on foot until the second half of the 20th century, and a traditional way of life lingered longer here than in other parts of the island. The west also has Crete's two most attractive towns, Chania and Rethymno, and some of the best beaches, ranging from pebbly coves to long swathes of golden sand.

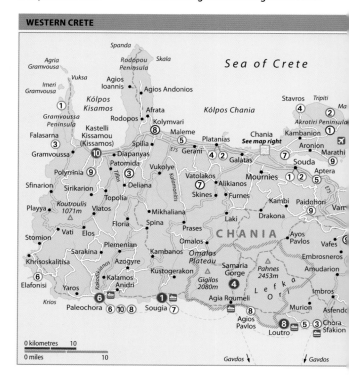

WESTERN CRETE

Previous pages The Dikteon Cave, said to be the birthplace of Zeus

An hour's walk away, the ruins of the ancient city-state of Lissos can be found, including a temple to the healing god Asclepius. It has a mosaic floor which dates from the 3rd century BC.

2 Rethymno

Rethymno is Crete's third-largest town (after Irakleio and Chania) and its most attractive, with an inner harbour overlooked by a huge, brooding Venetian fortress (the Fortezza), streets of old-fashioned Venetian mansions, and a palm-fringed esplanade along a sandy beach. Thanks to its nearby beaches, Rethymno has become a fully fledged resort town, with holiday hotels east of the city centre, and plenty of shops, restaurants, bars and cafés. It also has colourful early morning markets on Thursday and Saturday (see pp26–7).

The rugged coastline around Sougia

1 Sougia
MAP C4

Sougia is perfect for anyone in search of peace, quiet and isolation. Tourism is very low-key, with just a scattering of small pensions and guesthouses, tavernas and cafés. The town's beach is long and pebbly, and the water is sparklingly clear.

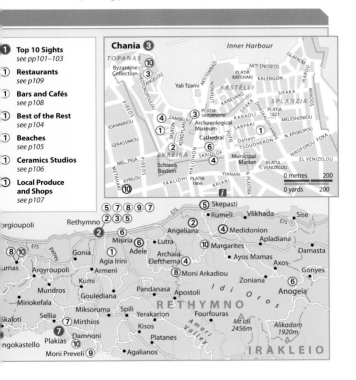

3 Chania

Chania, Crete's second-largest city, is built around a natural harbour that attracted many settlers over the millennia, from Minoans to Romans, Byzantines, Saracens, Venetians and Ottomans. The old town, a huddle of narrow streets, is well sown with bars, eateries, shops and museums. Chania has some of Crete's most spectacular scenery as a backdrop, with the slopes of the Lefka Ori (White Mountains) rising steeply a short way inland and dominating the entire southern horizon *(see pp20–21)*.

The mosque in the Old Port at Chania

4 Samaria Gorge

Taking its name from the tiny Venetian-era church of Osia Maria, this is probably Crete's most dramatic stretch of scenery. The gorge cuts its way through the Lefka Ori from the Omalos Plateau to the Libyan Sea, and narrows to a width of only a few arm widths at its narrowest point. The gorge lies within the Samaria National Park, a refuge for many rare birds, plants and mammals *(see pp30–31)*.

5 Frangokastello

MAP E4

A small "Castle of the Franks", actually built by the Venetians to defend this stretch of the south coast against pirate attacks *(see p46)*, gives this small resort its name. Frango-kastello has two separate sandy coves, and offers, by way of accommodation, small pensions and apartments. A handful of restaurants and cafés cater for visitors, and locally caught fish regularly features on the menus.

6 Paleochora

MAP B4

Paleochora stands on a peninsula between a long sandy bay to the northwest and an even longer, but pebblier beach to the southeast. Just beyond the village, on a cape, loom the ruined walls of Venetian fort Castel Selino, built to guard the harbour and coast but left to crumble after the Ottoman conquest. Paleochora is one of Crete's quieter resorts, with a low-key nightlife and a family atmosphere.

7 Plakias

MAP F4

Plakias's excellent beaches were overlooked by the holiday industry until the late 1980s, when the tiny fishing community became a strip of hotels, apartments, shops and restaurants. Plakias has plenty going for it, including attractive surrounding countryside, a long sweep of shingly sand, and other, even prettier beaches and palm-fringed coves within walking distance.

8 Loutro

MAP D4

Snugly hemmed in by cliffs rising steeply just inland, Loutro is one of the most charming spots on Crete. Dazzling white pensions and apartments sit above the tiny crescent-shaped beach. Accessible only on foot (by a precarious cliff path) or by boat from Chora Sfakion, Loutro is ideal for a laid-back holiday – without sandy beaches.

BANDIT COUNTRY

The Sfakia region lived by its own laws for generations, and vendettas between local families were not uncommon, even a couple of generations back. Prosperity and communications have tamed the region somewhat, but most Sfakiots still have an illicit firearm or two hidden away in the attic – and in the remoter parts, it seems that no road sign has escaped target practice.

9 Georgioupoli
MAP E3

Founded little over a century ago, this town was named in honour of Prince George, the then-governor of Crete. It is now a resort, with hotels stretching along the sandy beach. Georgioupoli attracts a less raucous clientele than resorts such as Malia and Chersonisos. At its heart is a town square, shaded by eucalyptus trees, while nearby a river meets the sea.

10 Kissamos
MAP B2

Formally known as Kastelli Kissamou, Crete's westernmost town is tucked away in a bay between the Rodopou and Gramvoussa peninsulas. There are several rarely visited ancient and medieval sites nearby, including Polyrrinia *(see p47)*, plus an excellent archaeological museum *(see p48)*. There are also pleasant (if un-exceptional by Cretan standards) beaches on either side of town.

Whitewashed houses in Loutro

A MORNING IN RETHYMNO

Begin your day at Plateia Tessera Martyron, where **Porta Guora** *(see p27)* – the only intact remnant of the Venetian city walls – leads into the old town. Pass through the gate and walk north along **Ethnikis Anistasis**, where the market bustles with stalls, open-fronted shops and cafés. This is a great place to buy herbs, honey and olive oil. This street ends beside the **Nerantzes Mosque**, converted from a Venetian church, as can be seen from the ornate northern portal. Its slender minaret can be seen from some distance.

At Nerantzes, turn left onto Vernardou and midway along, on your left, step into the **Historical and Folk Art Museum** *(see p50)*, displaying textiles and traditional costumes. Next, turn right on Epimenidou, then again right onto Arabatzoglou, which leads down to Petihaki, a small square where you'll find the **Rimondi Fountain** *(see p27)*, built in 1627 to supply the town with drinking water. Nearby, the elegant 16th-century **Loggia** *(see p27)* is a poignant reminder of Venice's reign.

Continue along Mesolongiou, past the Catholic church of St Anthony of Padua, then onto Himaras to the **Rethymno Archaeological Museum** *(see p49)*, which displays Neolithic, Minoan and Roman finds. Cross Katehaki to the **Fortezza** *(see p26)*. This fortress was built by the Venetians in 1573 to protect against invasion, but in the end it proved no match for the Ottomans, who merely skirted it to take the city. End with a seafood lunch at one of the quayside tavernas at the **Venetian Harbour**.

See map on pp100–101

Best of the Rest

 Monastery of Agia Irini
MAP F3 ▪ 28310 27791
▪ 9am–8pm daily

This 14th-century monastery is now a nunnery and also a centre for traditional weaving and needlework.

② **Akrotiri Peninsula**
MAP D2

Monks have been drawn to Crete's peninsulas – Akrotiri's best monasteries are the abandoned Moni Katholiko and the Venetian Moni Agias Triadas (Tzangarolon) *(see pp44–5)*.

③ **Chora Sfakion**
MAP D4

A major rendezvous point for excursion groups who arrive by boat having walked the Samaria Gorge. Once they have returned to their coaches, the town returns to its pleasant slumber.

④ **Ancient Eleftherna**
MAP G3 ▪ 8:30am–7pm daily

Founded in 700 BC, ancient Eleftherna was a powerful Dorian city. Having vanished from history, it is now being rediscovered by Greek archaeologists.

⑤ **Aptera**
MAP D2 ▪ 8:30am–3pm Tue–Sun

A Byzantine town built on the site of a Hellenistic city, remains here include Roman cisterns, Byzantine foundations, a Venetian monastery and an Ottoman fort.

⑥ **Anogeia**
MAP H4

Cafés and shops conceal Anogeia's embattled past, when it was a hotbed of resistance – first against the Ottomans, then the Germans.

 Souda Bay War Cemetery
MAP D2

The burial place of more than 1,500 Commonwealth soldiers who died in the Battle of Crete in May 1941.

⑧ **Moni Arkadiou**
MAP G4

This 16th-century monastery combines Cretan vernacular and Baroque architecture and includes an ornate Venetian church *(see pp36–7)*.

⑨ **Polyrrinia**
MAP B2

Wonderful views surround the broken walls and foundations of this ancient acropolis, upon which stands a ruined Venetian fortress *(see p47)*.

⑩ **Maritime Museum of Crete**
MAP A5 ▪ Akti Koundourioti, Chania
▪ 9am–5pm Mon–Sat, 10am–6pm Sun (Nov–Apr: 9am–3:30pm daily)
▪ Adm ▪ www.mar-mus-crete.gr

Navigational tools, model ships and naval equipment trace Crete's relationship with the sea in the Firkas fortress *(see p21)*.

Inside the Maritime Museum of Crete

Beaches

Balos
MAP B1

This pale-pink sand beach looks onto a shallow turquoise lagoon. Most visitors reach it by organized boat trips. Alternatively, drive along a pot-holed track from Kalyviani – a 4x4 jeep is essential.

The beach and lagoon at Balos

Platanias
MAP C2

This is the best long beach within easy reach of Chania, offering plenty of places to eat and drink. Platanias is Chania's after-dark summer play-ground, packed with bars and clubs.

3 Falasarna
MAP A2

This long sweep of yellow sand is one of the finest on the west coast. The archaeological site at the north end helps control development, but there are plenty of tavernas and places to stay midway along the beach.

4 Stavros
MAP D2

Quieter than Platanias, making it an attractive alternative for those seeking a little tranquillity. This lagoon-like bay on Akrotiri Peninsula featured in the film *Zorba the Greek*.

Glyka Nera (Sweet-water Beach)
MAP D4

A tiny patch of pebble and sand, Glyka Nera takes its name from the fresh, potable water which wells up wherever you dig. It is reachable only by scrambling along a rough path (part of the E4), or by boat from Loutro or Chora Sfakion. Naturists favour this beach.

Elafonisi
MAP A4

The beach opposite the island of Elafonisi on the west coast is one of Crete's best, with a long crescent of white sand and shallow turquoise water that quickly warms in summer. It is very popular and is often busy.

7 Sougia
MAP C4

Shaded in places by a line of tamarisk trees, Sougia is one of the last alternative resorts in Crete, with free camping and nudism at the beach's east end, but enough space for all persuasions along its mile-plus length.

Agios Pavlos
MAP F5

A popular day-trip from Agia Galini, Agios Pavlos's main cove is not as impressive as the west beach, which is approached by descending Crete's largest sand dune.

Preveli Finikas
MAP F5

The Kourtaliotis river meets the sea below Moni Preveli, where the green river, blue sea, Cretan palms and "Greek bamboo" (calamus reeds) create an oasis-like feel.

Damnoni
MAP F4

Damnoni's golden sands have been somewhat marred by insensitive hotel building. However, east of the main beach are two charming sandy coves, Ammoudaki and Mikro Ammoudaki, both popular with naturists.

See map on pp100–101

Ceramics Studios

Ceramic items at Tetraktis Studio

1 Tetraktis Studio
MAP D2 ▪ Verekynthos 6, Souda Chania ▪ www.tetraktis-studio.gr

Yiannis Vlavogilakis makes board games from ceramics – draughts, dominoes and solitaire – as well as tiles and dozens of drums.

2 Ourios Ceramics
MAP D2 ▪ Verekynthos 17, Souda Chania ▪ www.ouriosceramics.gr

Babis Magdalinos creates ceramic ornaments with decorative details inspired by Greek folk art, and innovative glazes made from recycled glass bottles.

3 Flakatoras Ceramics
MAP B5 ▪ Zampeliou 19, Chania ▪ www.flakatoras-ceramics.com

This family-run studio and shop makes and sells hand-painted cups, plates and tiles, plus quirky colourful ornaments such as model fish, snails and penguins.

4 Michael Laventzakis
MAP B6 ▪ Skrydlof 38, Chania ▪ www.laventzakisceramics.gr

With designs inspired by Greek folk art, this family business produces functional and decorative teapots, cups, bowls and plates in 16 colours.

5 Apostolakis
MAP C2 ▪ Maleme, 16 km (10 miles) W of Chania ▪ 28210 62438

Costas Apostolakis creates ceramic cups, bowls, jugs, vases and candle-holders glazed in warm shades of orange, red, blue or green.

6 Melody Ceramics
MAP B6 ▪ Betolo 27, Chania

Visit this studio and shop to purchase colourful handmade ceramics, including ornamental model boats, seagulls, flowers and pomegranates.

7 Vardaxis Ceramics
MAP P2 ▪ Panou Koronaiou 31, Rethymno

George Vardaxis's plates, bowls, vases and tiles are hand-painted. His family have been making them for generations – his grandfather has works displayed in Athens Greek Folk Art Museum.

Figurine, Ourios Ceramics

8 Terra-Cotta
MAP E3 ▪ Kournas ▪ www.terra-cotta.gr

This family-run business makes beautiful oven-proof, dishwasher-safe kitchenware – plates, bowls, goblets and jugs – in 12 different glaze colours.

9 Manousos Chalkiadakis
MAP D3 ▪ Paidochori ▪ www.greekceramics.gr

In a renovated 18th-century house, Manousos's studio is open daily to visitors. You can buy his handmade ceramics here, and he also runs one-day ceramics courses.

10 e+a ceramic studio
MAP G3 ▪ Margarites, 27 km (17 miles) E of Rethymno ▪ www.eaceramicstudio.com/wordpress

Margarites is known for its centuries-old potteries. In their studio, Ema and Aris create funky modern handcrafted tableware: cups, jugs and bowls.

See map on pp100–101

Local Produce and Shops

1 Moni Agia Triada
MAP D2 ▪ Akrotiri Peninsula
Visit Moni Agia Triada's monastery
(see p45), near Chania, then buy
extra-virgin olive oil and organic wine
made by the monks themselves.

2 Athos Workshop
**MAP G3 ▪ Angeliana, 23 km
(14 miles) E of Rethymno**
▪ www.athosworkshop.com
This small company
makes olive oil-based
soaps – visit to see
demonstrations and
to buy soaps, herbal
extracts and creams at
its shop.

**Soap, Athos
Workshop**

3 Astrikas Estate Biolea
MAP C2 ▪ Astrikas ▪ www.biolea.gr
In the hills behind Kolymvari, Biolea
offers guided tours of the mill, an
audio-visual presentation and olive-
oil tastings. It also sells organic
citrus-flavoured olive oil.

4 Paraschakis Olive Oil
**MAP G3 ▪ Melidoni
Geropotamou, 27 km (17 miles) E of
Rethymno ▪ www.paraschakis.gr**
This family-run farm offers an olive-
oil tour including the history of
olive-oil production, plus oil for sale.

5 Klados
**MAP G3 ▪ Skepasti, 25 km
(16 miles) E of Rethymno**
▪ www.kladoswinery.gr
Tours here include a walk through
the vineyard and a winemaking
presentation, followed by wine-
tasting (just four labels). There
is also the chance to buy bottles.

6 Agreco Farm
**MAP F3 ▪ Adele, 7 km (4 miles)
E of Rethymno ▪ www.agreco.gr**
Visit this welcoming farm shop to
purchase beautifully packaged,
locally-made Agreco olive oil, plus the
farm's own Eau de Grece toiletries.

7 Manousakis
**MAP C2 ▪ Vatolakos,
15 km (9 miles) SW of Chania**
▪ www.manousakiswinery.com
This boutique winery offers tours and
tastings, with an optional lunch, plus
excellent organic wine and *tsikoudia*
(a distillation of grape pomace called
raki elsewhere in Crete) to purchase.

8 Terra Creta
**MAP C2 ▪ Kolymvari, main
highway 24 km (15 miles) W of
Chania ▪ www.terracreta.gr**
This large-scale olive-oil
producer runs tours of the
mill followed by tastings and
a chance to buy its award-
winning extra-virgin olive oil
and balsamic vinegar.

9 Dourakis
MAP E3 ▪ Alikambos
▪ www.dourakiswinery.gr
Open for informative tours and
tastings, this award-winning winery
lies in the fertile Apokoronos region,
about halfway between Chania and
Rethymno, and produces nearly a
dozen reds, whites and rosés.

10 Abea Deli Shop
MAP A6 ▪ Skalidi 116, Chania
▪ www.abea.gr/en/deli-shop
Founded in 1889, Abea Deli stocks
its own olive oil and natural olive oil-
based soaps and cosmetics. Beautifully
packaged, they make fine gifts.

Items on display at Abea Deli Shop

Bars and Cafés

Tables outside Yannis Place, an old-fashioned ouzeri in Paleochora

① Kibar: To Monastiri Tou Karolou, Chania

MAP B6 ▪ Daliani 22

Kibar, in the courtyard of a former monastery, serves cocktails into the early hours. There are occasional DJ events, and even an art gallery.

② Sinagogi Bar, Chania

MAP A5 ▪ Alley off Kondylaki, Old Harbour

This popular bar is set in the large courtyard of a Venetian ruin that was once a synagogue. Corner sofas and quiet music provide a low-key vibe.

③ Fagotto Jazz Bar, Chania

MAP A6 ▪ Angelou 16

Chania's locals have been coming to Fagotto for a late-night drink, accompanied by occasional live jazz, since 1978. It is in Topahanas district, and may open only after 10pm.

④ Mylos, Platanias

MAP C2 ▪ Platanias Beach
▪ www.myloschania.com

A beachside club, Mylos is one of the prime summer-night destinations for local youth, with DJs and theme parties.

⑤ Garden of Ali Vafi, Rethymno

MAP Q2 ▪ Tzane Bouniali 65

In the courtyard of a wealthy Cretan Muslim merchant, this lantern-lit bar-restaurant offers drinks, snacks and hookah pipes, plus one weekly evening concert by established musicians.

⑥ Yannis Place, Paleochora

MAP B4 ▪ Venizelou 35

A traditional *kafeneio* on the town's main street. Don't expect a list of sophisticated cocktails; do expect authentic Cretan ambience.

⑦ Kafeneion O Platanos, Rethymno

MAP Q2 ▪ Plateia Petihaki

A rare authentic *kafeneio*, serving thimbles of Greek coffee and glasses of *tsikondia* (a strong spirit) to a clientele of venerable locals.

⑧ Meli, Rethymno

MAP Q2 ▪ Plateia Petihaki

The best ice cream in Rethymno old town, by far. No tables, but just sit or stand near the adjacent Rimondi Fountain for more cooling effect.

⑨ Cul de Sac, Rethymno

MAP Q2 ▪ Plateia Petihaki
▪ 28310 26914

Close to the Rimondi Fountain, Cul de Sac is the perfect place for people-watching over a coffee or a cocktail.

⑩ Nostos Club, Paleochora

MAP B4 ▪ Pebble Beach
▪ 69748 93355

This open-air affair is the best of the music bars along Pebble Beach. Rock, pop and dance music, usually DJd, from dusk until dawn, is interspersed with Cretan dancing to traditional *lyra* rhythms.

Restaurants

PRICE CATEGORIES
For a three-course meal for one with half
a bottle of wine (or equivalent meal),
taxes and extra charges.

€ under €25 ■ €€ €25–40 ■ €€€ over €40

Portes, Chania
**MAP A6 ■ Akti Papanikoli 1,
Neachora ■ 28210 76261 ■ €€**

An old-town favourite now in a seaside
setting, but preserving classic dishes
like aubergines imam or chickpea soup.
Plenty of desserts too. Try the cheese-
cake or sticky toffee pudding *(see p72)*.

2 Veneto, Rethymno
Epimenidou 4 ■ 28310 56634 ■ €€

Amid 14th-century vaults beneath
the Veneto Hotel, enjoy Cretan
specials such as fennelled snails and
couscous, stamnagathi and artichoke
fricasee, or *chtapodi krasato* atop
hummus and caramelised onions.

3 Avli, Rethymno
**MAP Q2 ■ Xanthoudidou 22
■ 28310 26213 ■ €€€**

Expect a changing menu of creative
Cretan recipes and simpler cheese-
based platters. Tables occupy a pretty
garden setting *(see p72)*.

Picturesque courtyard setting at Avli

4 Tamam, Chania
**MAP B5 ■ Zambeliou 49
■ 28210 96080 ■ €€**

Try Tanam's Cretan and Levantine
fusion dishes such as fennel fritters or
rabbit in rosemary-wine sauce *(see p72)*.

5 Ta Dyo Rou, Rethymno
**MAP Q2 ■ Panou Koronaiou 28,
Old Town ■ 6936 500392 ■ €**

This traditional wine-and-food shop
serves dishes such as artichokes
with broad beans, fennelled cuttlefish and stamnagathi (chicory).
Good bread and bulk wine.

6 Taverna tou Zisis, Rethymno
**Machis Kritis 63, Misiria
■ 28310 28814 ■ €**

On the old Irakleio highway, 4 km
(2 miles) east of Rethymno, Zisis'
charcoal-grilled lamb and chicken
dishes are worth the trip from town.

7 Plateia, Mirthios
**MAP F4 ■ Mirthios village
■ 28320 31560 ■ €**

Traditional Cretan food, friendly staff
and superb sea views guarantee
diners a good time *(see p74)*.

8 Methexi Paleochora
**MAP B4 ■ Palaiochora
■ 28230 41431 ■ €€**

Open most of the year, Methexi serves
generous dishes such as lambs-liver
roulade and *askolymbri* (golden thistle).

9 Patrelantonis, Marathi
**MAP E2 ■ On Akrotiri Peninsula
beach ■ 28210 63337 ■ €€**

Patrelantonis is much loved by locals
for its excellent fish and seafood
dishes, served at tables on a wooden
deck directly above the beach.

10 Kali Kardia, Kournas
**MAP E3 ■ Kournas village
■ 28250 96278 ■ €**

Delicious home-grown and organic
fare. The sausages are locally
renowned, and the lamb is excellent.

See map on pp100–101

TOP 10 Eastern Crete

Crete's far east sees fewer holiday-makers, mainly due to its distance from the island's airports. The area's largest town Agios Nikolaos, however, is already a thriving holiday resort, and Crete's most exclusive hotel and villa complexes can be found around Elounda. The east also has good beaches, notably the famous palm beach at Vaï, and Minoan ruins at Gournia, Mochlos and Zakros.

Pristine waters around Elounda

1 Elounda
MAP N4

Elounda is Crete's most expensive resort area, with many exclusive villa and hotel complexes, several of which have private beaches. The simple village has a cluster of shops and restaurants around a small fishing harbour. In summer, boats depart daily on trips to Spinalonga, the Venetian fortress-island.

EASTERN CRETE

Top 10 Sights
see pp110–13

Places to Eat
see p119

Bars and Cafés
see p118

Best of the Rest
see p114

Beaches
see p115

Photo Locations
see p116

Local Products
see p117

Remains of Spinalonga's fortress

2 Spinalonga
MAP N4

The fortifications covering this small, rocky island at the entry to the Gulf of Mirabello were built by the Venetians in 1579 to control the approaches to this natural harbour. Venice managed to hang on to Spinalonga for half a century after the fall of the rest of Crete to the Ottomans, and it was surrendered only in 1715. Used as a leper colony during the first half of the 20th century, its buildings are now dilapidated.

3 Ierapetra
MAP N6

Ierapetra is the largest town on the southeast coast. Aside from a tiny old quarter, it is rather dull, but has a good, long beach of grey sand and the distinction of receiving more hours of sunshine per year than anywhere else in Europe. Tomatoes and cucumbers are grown all year round in the surrounding farmlands. Ierapetra became an important Dorian Greek settlement in the 8th century BC, and by the 2nd century BC, it was the largest city-state on the island. Under the Romans, it was an important seaport; the Venetians built a fortress to defend the harbour. Today, the main sight is the archaeological museum.

4 Siteia
MAP Q4

Siteia looks surprisingly modern but was founded in the 4th century, when a thriving Byzantine city stood here. In the 14th century, it was damaged by earthquakes and sacked by pirates, and its fortunes waned. It was not until the late 1800s that Siteia became an important commercial centre. Its picturesque harbour is overlooked by a Venetian fortress and an Archae-ological Museum *(see p49)*. Siteia is an important centre for the production of quality Cretan wines.

Palm-lined promenade at Siteia

THE CAVES OF CRETE
About 5,000 caverns and potholes riddle the island's mountain slopes. Grottoes have yielded fascinating relics of the ancient world, indicating that Crete was inhabited for thousands of years before the rise of the Minoan civilization. Only a handful have been fully charted, and thousands more remain to be fully explored and mapped.

 Makrygialos
MAP Q5

Makrygialos is the most popular holiday resort on Crete's south-eastern coast, with a long, straggling array of small pensions, hotels and tavernas stretching along a crescent of windswept, gently shelving sand and pebble beach, which is the best in this part of the island.

 Zakros Gorge
MAP R5

The Zakros Gorge is known locally as the Valley of the Dead because the caves in its limestone walls were used as tombs in Roman times. The gorge runs from the peaceful village of Ano ("upper") Zakros to Kato ("lower") Zakros on the sea, near an ancient Minoan palace site excavated in 1961. It is a beautiful hour-and-a-quarter hike uphill (allow an hour to walk back down) *(see also p65)*.

 Dikteon Cave
MAP M5

According to ancient Greek myths, this mossy cavern filled with strange limestone formations was the cradle of the greatest Olympian god, Zeus.

Rock formations in the Dikteon Cave

Rhea, Zeus's mother, supposedly hid the young godling from his father, Kronos, here. Bronze figurines and Minoan double axes found in the cave are on show in Irakleio Archaeological Museum. The site is also often referred to as the Psychro Cave.

 **Agios Nikolaos**
MAP N4

Set by the Gulf of Mirabello, Agios Nikolaos has the most attractive location of any town in eastern Crete. It is built around an inner lagoon, Voulismeni, surrounded by palm trees and pleasant cafés. Modern hotels and apartments now dwarf the surviving older buildings, but it is still a place of considerable charm. There are two small town beaches, and boats take holiday-makers to larger beaches nearby.

The town takes its name from the tiny 11th-century church of Agios Nikolaos (which now stands in the grounds of the Minos Palace Hotel).

9 Vaï
MAP R4

The beach at Vaï is famous for having the only wild palm grove in Europe. It is believed that Arab sailors planted the trees during historical times. However, both claims are spurious, as groves of this variety can be found around Crete, and elsewhere in the Aegean. The species, Phoenix Theoprasti, was first described by the 4th-century-BC botanist, Theophrastos, in whose honour it was named. Today, the palm trees are fenced off and protected. The beach becomes overcrowded in high season, and it is better to visit outside the busiest summer months.

10 Lasithi
MAP M4

The so-called "Plain of Windmills" is a high plain of fertile farmland surrounded by bare limestone hills. Its nickname is misleading, though. Nowadays, rusting metal derricks outnumber the famed white-sailed windmills that once dotted the plateau in their hundreds. However, Lasithi is still well worth a visit for the spectacular drive through the mountains and the glimpses it offers of the traditional Cretan way of life.

Panorama of Agios Nikolaos

A DRIVE IN EASTERN CRETE

This 200-km (125-mile) round trip from **Agios Nikolaos** can be made in one full day, or over two days, with an overnight stop at Zakros. From Agios Nikolaos, take the coastal highway east to **Gournia** (see pp34–5) to explore the Minoan archaeological site. Continue east to **Siteia** (see p111), founded by the Byzantines, destroyed in the 14th century and rebuilt by a local *pasha* (Ottoman governor) in the 19th century. It has a picturesque harbour, where you might stop for coffee, and an **Archaeological Museum** (see p49) displaying Minoan treasures.

Proceed east to **Moni Toplou** (see p45), a 14th-century fortified monastery. Visit the monastery church to see the icons, and to buy olive oil from the monks. Continue to **Vaï** beach, backed by its famous palm forest, now a conservation area, on Crete's east coast. Lined with parasols and sun beds, this sandy beach is one place you must have a swim. Once refreshed, head south to **Ano Zakros**, then turn left and drive down a narrow winding road to the seaside village of **Kato Zakros**, with its pebble-and-sand beachfront lined by informal tavernas. Stop for a late lunch, or even stay the night. After Zakros, head via the scenic Ziros plateau to Crete's south coast, through **Makrygialos**, another remote yet worthwhile beach resort, and west to seaside **Ierapetra** (see p111). Unlike most Cretan coastal towns, this resort's economy is based on farming rather than on tourism. From here, it's a 32-km (20-mile) drive back to Agios Nikolaos.

See map on pp110–11

Best of the Rest

 Kritsa
MAP N5

Overlooked by Mount Kastelleos, Kritsa stands at the edge of a wide, fertile plain and is regarded as one of Crete's most important craft centres.

2 Praisos
Based on clay statuettes and inscriptions found here, archaeologists believe it was a post-Minoan Eteocretan city *(see p43)*.

3 Cretan Olive Oil Farm
MAP N4 ▪ Agios Nikolaos
▪ www.cretanoliveoilfarm.com
Visit here to learn about traditional olive-oil production, and sign up to open-air cookery and pottery lessons.

 Lithines
MAP Q5

Named after its founders, the noble Byzantine Litinos clan, Lithines has two 15th-century churches, Agios Athanasios and Gennisi tis Panagias.

Ancient ruins at Lato

 Lato
MAP N4

Lato was a Dorian Greek city that flourished between the 7th and 3rd centuries BC. With massive stone walls, it offers fine views over the Gulf of Mirabello. Modern-day Agios Nikolaos was Lato's port.

Toplou Monastery, a local landmark

 Moni Toplou
This fortified monastery was founded in the 14th century. Its massive walls were built to protect it from pirates *(see p45)*.

7 Roussa Ekklisia
MAP R5

This pretty village is worth visiting for its superb view of Siteia bay. Large plane trees shade the village square, nurtured by the spring which flows from under the medieval Agios Nikolaos church.

 Moni Kapsa
MAP Q6 ▪ 8:30am–midday & 4–7pm

A monastery that seems to merge into the cliffs, with the mummified body of a monk in its chapel.

9 Pefki Gorge
MAP P5

An enjoyable 4-hour walk from Pefki to Makrygialos will take hikers along a dry river bed of white pebbles that runs through a pine-lined canyon with interesting rock formations.

10 Mochlos
MAP P4

East of Agios Nikolaos, Mochlos is a sleepy fishing hamlet. Just off shore, a tiny island (also called Mochlos) was home to an ancient Minoan settlement – excavations have uncovered superb gold jewellery and precious vases.

→ *See map on pp110–11*

Beaches

 Siteia
MAP Q4

Unlike most larger Cretan coastal towns, Siteia has a good beach on its doorstep that is great for windsurfing.

2 Xerokampos
MAP R5

A tiny hamlet with a series of small, sandy east-facing coves. One of the few coastal areas not overrun by tourists, but offering facilities.

3 Kouremenos
MAP R4

The strong breezes at Kouremenos make it a popular windsurfing spot, with best conditions during summer, usually in the afternoons.

4 Makrygialos
MAP Q5

The best beach on the southeast coast. A long strip of sand interspersed with pebbles shelves guiding you gently into deeper water.

5 Myrtos
MAP N6

An amiably unpretentious farming and fishing village with a long, south-facing shingle beach, which is far less crowded than most in eastern Crete, even in high summer.

 Agia Fotia
MAP R4

The best beach between Makrygialos and Ierapetra, this sheltered sandy cove, backed by pine-forested hills, makes a great swim-and-lunch stop.

 Chionia
MAP R4

This beach has a European Blue Flag for clean sand and water, as well as ample choice in tavernas just inland.

 Kato Zakros
MAP R5

At the foot of the Zakros Gorge, Kato Zakros has a crescent of sand and a pebble beach, with a small fishing harbour and a handful of pensions and tavernas.

The waterfront at Kato Zakros

 Milatos
MAP N4

A pebbly beach which is surprisingly uncrowded compared with the teeming resorts only a few kilometres to the west.

 Voulisma
MAP P5

This beautiful sandy cove, the best of several east of the resort of Istro, offers sunbeds and sometimes a light surf in which to play.

The azure waters of Voulisma beach

Photo Locations

 Vaï Sand Beach
MAP R4

The best spot for photographing this stunning beach, lined with straw umbrellas and sloping into shallow turquoise waters, is from the viewing platform on the hill at the south end.

 Vaï Palm Groves
Making up Europe's largest palm grove, the centuries-old date palms that back Vaï beach give it an exotic atmosphere. Wander underneath the towering trees for close-up shots (see p113).

 Spinalonga
This Venetian island fortress offers visitors many excellent viewpoints for taking photographs. It looks most impressive seen from aboard a boat as you approach the island's shore (see p111).

4 Agios Nikolaos
The centrepiece of this town is Voulismeni, a former fresh-water lake that is now joined to the sea by a narrow channel to form the inner harbour. The best viewpoint is from the road above the lake (see pp112–13).

5 Lasithi Windmills
High up on the Lasithi Plateau, you'll find many windmills – some of stone, some whitewashed and several restored, with their white sails turning (see p113).

 Dikteon Cave
This cave complex features an impressive lower chamber, which contains a small lake and is filled with beautifully lit stalactites and stalagmites (see p112).

 Zakros Gorge
Follow the path through this imposing steep-sided rocky gorge to descend at Kato Zakros, on the coast. On the way, look out for orchids, goats and buzzards (see p112).

8 Pefki Gorge
MAP Q5

Inland, north of Makrygialos, this gorge is known for its natural springs and streams, and for the fragrant pine trees that give it its name.

9 Chrisi Island
MAP N6

Accessed by daily summer excursion boats that sail from Ierapetra, this uninhabited island is made up of sand dunes and characterful, centuries-old juniper trees, giving way to a turquoise blue sea.

10 Ierapetra Harbour
This little south-coast port is filled with traditional wooden fishing boats, painted in white, blue and red, and equipped with buoys and nets. The castle serves as a backdrop (see p111).

 Windmills on the Lasithi Plateau

Local Products

 Cretan Olive Oil Farm
This farm has a shop selling its own excellent extra-virgin olive oil, olives and olive paté, sun-dried tomatoes, fig jam and handmade soaps. Ideal for a picnic *(see p114)*.

2 Votania Pure Herbs of Crete
MAP P5 ■ Kavousi beach, 26 km (16 miles) E of Agios Nikolaos
■ www.votania.com
Votania grows organic sage, oregano, thyme, rosemary, lavender and mint, and then sells the dried herbs for cooking, teas and cosmetics.

3 Art on Olive Wood
MAP N4 ■ Ikosiogdois Oktovriou 22, Agios Nikolaos
■ www.artonolivewood.com
Since 1985, this lovely workshop has been crafting beautiful objects, including ornate candle holders and elegant figurines of trees, boats and animals made from olive wood.

4 Terra Zakros
MAP R5 ■ Ano Zakros
■ www.sitiaterrazakros.gr
This store sells extra-virgin olive oil – awarded silver at the London International Olive Oil Competition 2016 and Athena International Oil Competition 2017 – as well as honey, herbs, wine and *raki* made by local producers.

5 Hatzis Leather
MAP M4 ■ E Venizelou 58 and Eleftherias 17, Chersonisos
■ www.hatzisleather.com
Visit this wonderful workshop (which was founded in 1960) and two shop-fronts for gorgeous handmade leather bags, sandals, belts and accessories, all made with classic Crete designs.

6 Street Market
MAP N6 ■ Psilinaki, Ierapetra
Every Saturday morning, local farmers and market gardeners set up stalls selling fresh seasonal produce at Ierapetra's street market.

7 Si-Mel Savidakis
MAP Q4 ■ Gela, Siteia
■ www.toplou-honey.com
This place is run by a bee-keeping family. It offers interesting tours and sells its own honey, royal jelly, pollen and *rakomelo* (raki flavoured with honey, to be served hot).

8 Daedalus
MAP M5 ■ Kritsa
■ www.daedalushop.com
This souvenir shop sells a range of contemporary handmade jewellery, ceramics and loom bags, plus *kilim* rugs with traditional motifs.

Colourful ceramic items at Daedalus

9 Myrtos Village
MAP N6
One of the original south-coast hippy hang-outs, Myrtos has boutiques selling clothing, jewellery and leather-canvas bags, both on the beach esplanade and inland. Boukamvilia and Soul's Art are both worth a visit.

10 Olive
MAP Q5 ■ Makrygialos
A small shop near the Sunwing Hotel stocking locally produced quality olive oil, honey, natural olive oil-based cosmetics and essential oils. Ideal for gifts or trip mementos.

See map on pp110–11

Bars and Cafés

① Alexandros Rooftop Bar, Agios Nikolaos
MAP N4 ■ Kondylaki 4

This popular bar serves cocktails at tables with flickering oil lamps and offers romantic views down onto Lake Voulismeni.

② Café-Snack Bar Vaï
MAP R4 ■ On the beach

In a beautiful setting behind the palm trees on the beach, this café and snack bar offers coffee, drinks, nibbles and ice cream prepared from fresh milk.

③ Epico Café Bar, Plaka
MAP N4 ■ On the beach

Offering fine views of Spinalonga island across the bay, this informal café and wine bar serves chilled beers, freshly squeezed juices, coffee, wine and nibbles.

④ Kaaren's, Elounda
MAP N4 ■ Akti Poseidonos 47
■ 28410 41709

This café-bar has wonderful views of the sea and serves delicious sandwiches, wraps, home-made sausages and a range of cocktails. Not open for dinner (see p76).

Selection of meze at Kaaren's

⑤ Ammoudi Club, Agios Nikolaos
MAP N4 ■ Ammoudi Cove ■ www.ammoudiclub.com

Combining a fashionable beach bar and sun beds for hire with a slick café-restaurant hosting guest DJs, Ammoudi is a popular waterside summer venue, by day or night.

Lively night-time scene at Puerto Bar

⑥ Puerto Café-Bar, Agios Nikolaos
MAP N4 ■ Akti Koundourou 9
■ 28410 22850

Enjoy drinks and cocktails at this harbourfront café-bar with great views from its terrace. After dark, retreat indoors as the music begins.

⑦ Veterano, Ierapetra
MAP N6 ■ Plateia Eleftherias
■ 28420 26136

This fashionable terrace café and bakery is ideal for a leisurely breakfast and just as good for a sundowner.

⑧ Café Olympio, Makrygialos
MAP P5 ■ Makrygialos Harbour
■ 28430 52135

Overlooking the small harbour from under tamarisks, this relaxing café-bar offers full breakfasts, salads, tasty snacks, draught beer and cocktails.

⑨ Mitsakakis, Siteia
MAP Q4 ■ Karamanli 6

This seafront café is renowned for its home-made Greek desserts, as well as for its excellent ice cream.

⑩ Amnesia, Kato Zakros
MAP R5 ■ Seafront

All-day beach café/snack bar with a difference: great ice creams, drinks and beers with accompanying nibbles. May get livelier after dark.

Places to Eat

1 **Paradosiako, Agios Nikolaos**

MAP N4 ▪ Akti Themistokleous 9, Europa Cove ▪ 28410 21666 ▪ €

A rare find here: an affordable, savoury seaside *mezedopoleio*, where diners tick off their choices on the combined menu/order sheet.

2 **Kalliotzina, Koutsouras**

MAP P5 ▪ Seafront ▪ 28430 51207 ▪ Closed Nov–Apr ▪ €

This taverna serves good home-cooked meals at outside tables overhung by tamarisk trees *(see p75).*

3 **Agkistri (Nikolaos O Psaras)**

MAP R4 ▪ Agkathia ▪ 28430 61598 ▪ €

Village-centre taverna between Moni Toplou and local beaches that is un-rivalled for its grilled fish straight off Nikolas' boat, and a limited number of casserole dishes and starters.

4 **The Ferryman, Elounda**

MAP N4 ▪ Akti Olountos ▪ 28410 41230 ▪ €€

With views across the water to the island of Spinalonga, this seafood taverna has won many awards. Expect dishes based on fresh local ingredients *(see p73).*

5 **Akrogiali, Kato Zakros**

MAP R5 ▪ On the beach ▪ 28430 26893 ▪ €

A relaxed spot overlooking the beach, Akrogiali serves drinks, seafood and grilled meat.

Beachside tables at Akrogiali

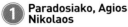

PRICE CATEGORIES

For a three-course meal for one with half a bottle of wine (or equivalent meal), taxes and extra charges.

€ under €25   €€ €25–40   €€€ over €40

6 **Poulis, Elounda**

MAP N4 ▪ Harbourfront ▪ 28410 41451 ▪ Closed Nov–Apr ▪ €€

Poulis has mainly Cretan/Greek specialities with some international dishes. It also serves a wide selection of grilled seafood, along-side a reasonable wine list *(see p73).*

7 **Levante, Ierapetra**

MAP N6 ▪ Stratigou Samouil 36 ▪ 28420 80585 ▪ €

Next to the Ierapetra beach, Levante is a great place at which to sample regional fare such as *omathies* – sausages stuffed with rice and offal – and *chochlioi bourbouristi* – snails sautéed in lemon and rosemary.

8 **Stratos Restaurant, Makrygialos**

MAP P5 ▪ Kalamokanias Beach ▪ 28430 52357 ▪ €€

Traditional Cretan dishes, plus the odd grilled fish, are served here by a well-travelled couple who use plenty of herbs and spices in their food.

9 **Ta Kochylia, Mochlos**

MAP P4 ▪ Mochlos Seafront ▪ 28430 94432 ▪ €

The oldest (from 1902) local taverna offers seafood, vegetarian platters and daily-changing casseroles, as well as views of Mochlos islet.

10 **Balcony, Siteia**

MAP Q4 ▪ Foundalidou 19 ▪ 28430 25084 ▪ €€€

Located in an elegant town house, this restaurant serves Cretan cuisine with Asian and Mexican influences. It has an impressive wine list with plenty of local options *(see p72).*

See map on pp110–11 ←

Streetsmart

Vine-filled alleyway in the
Old Town, Chania

Getting To and Around Crete

Arriving by Air

Crete is served by three international airports: **Irakleio** (HER), **Chania** (CHQ) and **Siteia** (JSH). The former lies 5 km (3 miles) east of Irakleio and is connected by bus and taxi. Chania Airport lies 15 km (9 miles) east of Chania, on the Akrotiri Peninsula, and it also has both bus and taxi links. Siteia Airport is a mere 1.5 km (1 mile) from the city centre, with only taxi or walking access.

From Easter until late October, many airlines serve Crete. Budget airlines, such as **EasyJet**, **Ryanair**, **Thomson** and **Jet2** fly in from several airports in the UK, while **British Airways** serves Irakleio from London Gatwick. Greek carriers **Olympic Air**, **Sky Express** and **Aegean Airlines** link Crete with other Greek destinations, as does **Ryanair**. Charter airlines owned by large package-holiday companies fly to Chania and Irakleio from most airports in the UK and from large mainland EU cities. In winter, visitors have to travel to Crete via Athens.

There are regular internal flights to either Chania and Irakleio from other Greek islands, including Santorini, Kos and Rhodes.

Arriving by Sea

Crete has two main ferry ports, Irakleio and Chania, both on the north coast. The port of Irakleio lies opposite the city centre, while Chania's port is at Souda, 7 km (4 miles) east of Chania, to which it is connected by bus.

Daily overnight ferries with comfortable cabins depart from Athens port Piraeus for both Irakleio (the journey time is 9 hrs) and Chania (the journey time is 8 hrs 30 mins). Both routes are jointly operated by **Blue Star Ferries** and **ANEK Lines**. In addition, Irakleio is also served by **Minoan Lines**. It is possible to take cars on these ferries.

ANEK Lines also runs a slow but cheap, twice-a-week service between Irakleio and Rhodes (journey time 14.5 hours), stopping at Karpathos.

In summer (Apr–Oct), there are also daily high-speed catamarans connecting Crete to the Cycladic Islands. Both **Hellenic Seaways** and **SeaJets** run a service from Irakleio to Santorini, Naxos, Paros and Mykonos; SeaJets also sails to Ios. The journey from Irakleio to Santorini takes just 1 hr 45 mins.

Travelling by Car

The main cities along Crete's northern coast – Chania, Irakleio, Agios Nikolaos and Rethymno – are connected by a fast, dual-carriageway motorway known as the Crete National Road (A90). The eastern section, from Chersonisos to Siteia, is narrower and twistier, with much of it still under construction.

Crete is a large island, and distances are greater than you might imagine from looking at a map.

Due to the nature of the landscape, with rugged mountains and deep gorges, the road network remains scanty in parts. Roads through the mountainous interior are generally narrow and twisty, and some are poorly surfaced. In rural areas, you may find livestock on the roads, so caution is advised. Villages along the south coast tend to be poorly connected by road – in some cases, it is easier to travel by boat.

There are local and international car rental companies at the airports and ferry ports, and in all major towns and resorts. Renting on the spot is more expensive than booking in advance.

During peak season, finding a parking space in the busy towns of Chania, Irakleio and Rethymno can be a problem. It is best to park outside the centre and walk in, or use a fee lot.

Travelling by Bus

The cities of Chania, Rethymno and Irakleio are connected by fast and comfortable hourly buses. Some of these buses continue east to Agios Nikolaos. The rest of the island is also served by bus, so it is possible to reach even remote villages. Services may be infrequent – sometimes only one bus per day – and the route may be long and poorly surfaced.

Buses are operated by the **KTEL Chania-Rethymno** and the **KTEL**

Irakleio and Lasithi. English-language time-tables, usually available from local tourist offices, are not always reliable.

Travelling by Taxi

Taxis are inexpensive and operate both in towns and on longer journeys between towns and villages. Short trips are metered, but for longer trips there is usually a fixed price – agree it before setting off. Most drivers speak some English.

Travelling by Local Boat

The south-coast villages of Paleochora, Sougia, Agia Roumeli, Loutro and Chora Sfakion are connected by boat, but not by road. In summer, small ferries operated by **Anendyk** cover this route daily.

Travelling by Motor-bike or Scooter

Two-wheeled transport is popular with summer visitors. However, caution should be exercised – accidents among visitors, especially inexperienced riders, are common. Helmets are compulsory, and it is also a good idea to wear long trousers and a jacket.

Travelling by Bicycle

Cycling is becoming increasingly popular on Crete. Away from the north coast, there are hundreds of miles of rural roads and farm tracks, ideal for mountain-biking.

Various companies arrange guided and non-guided cycling tours and holidays, and bicycles to hire are available in all the main resorts.

Cycling is best enjoyed in spring (Apr–May) and autumn (Sep–Oct); mid-summer is feasible only at high altitudes.

If you're looking for a challenge, consider taking part in the **Tour of Crete**, a six-day race across the island held each May.

Travelling on Foot

The old towns of Chania, Rethymno and Irakleio are mostly pedestrian-only and a joy to explore on foot. Some of Crete's most rewarding beaches are quite isolated, and you will have to trek some distance to reach them.

Moving into the interior, Crete offers fantastic landscapes for hiking. The island has several mountains over 2,000 m (6,500 ft), posing a real challenge to hardened walkers and climbers, while its numerous gorges are perfect for novices who prefer easier walking. Organized hiking tours and holidays are very popular.

The E4 European long-distance path (*see p65*) crosses the entire island, running from Kissamos (Kastelli) on the west coast to Kato Zakros on the east.

The best seasons for hiking are spring and autumn.

DIRECTORY

ARRIVING BY AIR

Aegean Airlines
w aegeanair.com

British Airways
w britishairways.com

Chania Airport
c 28210 83800
w chania-airport.com

EasyJet
w easyjet.com

Irakleio Airport
c 2810 397800
w heraklion-airport.info

Jet2
w jet2.com

Olympic Air
w olympicair.com

Ryanair
w ryanair.com

Thomson Airlines
w thomson.co.uk/flight
c 0203 451 2688

ARRIVING BY SEA

ANEK Lines
w anek.gr

Blue Star Ferries
w bluestarferries.com

Hellenic Seaways
w hellenicseaways.gr

Minoan Lines
w minoan.gr

SeaJets
w seajets.gr

TRAVELLING BY BUS

KTEL Chania–Rethymno
c 28210 93052, 28310 22785
w e-ktel.com

KTEL Irakleio and Lasithi
c 2810 246530
w ktelherlas.gr

TRAVELLING BY LOCAL BOAT

Anendyk
w anendyk.gr

TRAVELLING BY BICYCLE

Tour of Crete
w tourofcrete.com

Practical Information

Passports and Visas

Visitors from outside the European Economic Area (EEA), European Union (EU) and Switzerland need a valid passport to travel to Crete, as do UK visitors; most other EU nationals require only a valid identity card. Citizens of Canada, the USA, Australia and New Zealand do not need visas for stays of up to 90 days as long as their passport is valid for 6 months beyond the date of entry. For longer stays, a visa is necessary and must be obtained in advance from the Greek embassy. For details and useful information, check the website of the Greek **Ministry of Foreign Affairs**.

Most countries have embassies in Athens – including **Canada**, the **US**, the **UK** and **Australia** – and can provide consular services. Irakleio also has a **UK Vice Consulate**.

Customs and Immigration

Visitors from the EU are not subject to customs formalities on alcohol and tobacco, as long as they keep within the following limits in their personal baggage: 800 cigarettes, 400 cigarillos, 200 cigars, 1 kg (2 lb) of tobacco, 10 litres of spirits, 90 litres of wine and 110 litres of beer.

Visitors from non-EU countries are permitted to carry the following allowances in their personal luggage: 200 cigarettes or 250 g (8 oz) of smoking tobacco, 1 litre of spirits, 4 litres of wine, as well as 16 litres of beer. If carrying prescription drugs, you should also bring a copy of the prescription itself, preferably the original container and label. The unauthorized export of antiquities and art is a serious offence.

Travel Safety Advice

Get up-to-date travel safety information from the **UK Foreign and Commonwealth Office**, the **US Department of State** and the **Australian Department of Foreign Affairs and Trade**.

Travel Insurance

Before travelling, you are advised to take out comprehensive travel insurance covering yourself for private medical treatment and for evacuation and repatriation, if necessary, as well as for loss or theft of your belongings and expenses incurred due to delayed or cancelled flights. Make sure your policy will pay for medical and hospital fees direct, and that it will cover you for holiday activities such as trekking, scuba diving, riding and motorcycling, as well as for personal liability in the event of damage to rented cars or motorcycles. Most annual policies only cover trips of up to 30 days; for longer stays it is better to opt for a one-off policy.

Health

A European Health Insurance Card (EHIC) covers any necessary medical treatment for EU citizens in Greek public hospitals. However, it is much better to make sure your insurance covers private treatment. If hospital treatment is necessary, then go to the **University General Hospital of Irakleio** (PAGNI), which also has a medical school.

Greek pharmacists can provide comprehensive advice on minor ailments and injuries, and they can dispense a wide range of remedies. They usually speak English. Most pharmacies, marked by a green cross sign, are open only Monday to Friday from 8am to 2:30pm, but when closed, they have a sheet on the door listing nearby duty pharmacies (limited evening and weekend hours).

There are private medical clinics in all the main towns, and many doctors speak good English. Dentists are proficient and can be found in major towns, including Irakleio, Agios Nikolaos, Rethymno, Siteia, Ierapetra and Chania. Visitors should be aware that consultations and treatments at the doctor and dentist must be paid for in cash. Dental fees are comparable to a UK NHS dentist.

Emergency Services

There are a number of emergency services numbers in Crete, including those for **ambulance**, **police**, **tourist police**, **hospitals**, and **SOS Doctors**.

Personal Security

Crete has a very low crime rate and is one of the safest holiday destinations in the world. However, thefts from tourists do occur. Take sensible precautions, including locking rental cars and hotel rooms, and keeping passports, tickets and spare cash in hotel safes. Never leave anything valuable in the car, even a locked one; the environs of Irakleio's Archaeological Museum especially, are hunting grounds for opportunistic thieves. If you have had things stolen, or have cause to complain about restaurants, tour guides or taxi drivers, you should immediately contact the local "tourist police" – they speak several foreign languages, including English. Alternatively, go to the police stations in **Chania** or **Irakleio**.

Travellers with Specific Needs

Crete is generally not well equipped to cater for disabled travellers. Some of the modern resort hotels have rooms designed for guests with impaired mobility, and visitors with disabilities are entitled to free entry to state-run museums and archaeological sites.

Sources of Information

The **Greek National Tourism Organisation** (GNTO) has offices located all around the world. On Crete, Irakleio has an official GNTO office that will provide visitors with useful maps, bus timetables and lists of things to see. The **Region of Crete** website is also full of helpful information.

Trips and Tours

Agencies in Rethymno, Irakleio, Agios Nikolaos and Chania can organize a range of day trips to various beaches or to important sights on the island, such as the Samaria Gorge or Ancient Knossos.

Visitors will also find that several outdoor adventure sports companies offer excellent hiking, mountain-biking, sea-kayaking and sailing trips, especially in Central Crete *(see p94)*.

DIRECTORY

PASSPORTS AND VISAS

Australian Embassy
Kifisias & Alexandras Avenue, Ambelokipi, 11523 Athens
W greece.embassy.gov.au

Canadian Embassy
Ethnikis Antistaseos 48, Halandri, 15231 Athens
W greece.gc.ca

Ministry of Foreign Affairs
W mfa.gr/en/visas

UK Embassy
Ploutarchou 1, 10675 Athens
W gov.uk/government/world/organisations/british-embassy-athens

UK Vice Consulate
MAP T1 ■ Candia Tower, Thalita 17, 5th Floor
C 2810 224012
W gov.uk/government/world/organisations/british-vice-consulate-crete

US Embassy
Vasilissis Sofias 91, 10160 Athens
W gr.usembassy.gov

TRAVEL SAFETY ADVICE

Australian Department of Foreign Affairs and Trade
W dfat.gov.au
W smartraveller.gov.au

UK Foreign and Commonwealth Office
W gov.uk/foreign-travel-advice

US Department of State
W travel.state.gov

HEALTH

University General Hospital of Irakleio
MAP K3 ■ Voutes, 71110 Irakleio

EMERGENCY SERVICES

Ambulance
C 166

Hospitals
C 1434

Police
C 100

SOS Doctors
C 1016

Tourist Police
C 171

PERSONAL SECURITY

Chania Police Station
MAP D2 ■ Leoforos Irakleiou 23, 73100
C 28210 25850

Irakleio Police Station
MAP K3 ■ Agiou Artemiou 1, 71601 Nea Alikarnassos
C 2810 274110

SOURCES OF INFORMATION

Greek National Tourism Organisation
W visitgreece.gr

Region of Crete
W incrediblecrete.gr

Currency and Banking

Greece uses the euro (€), which is divided into 100 cents. Banknotes are in denominations of €5, €10, €20, €50, €100, €200 and €500, and coins are 1c, 2c, 5c, 10c, 20c and 50c (lepta), and €1 and €2.

The easiest way to get cash is to use an ATM – these are widely available in all the main towns and resorts. Credit cards are accepted at larger hotels, restaurants and shops. Alternatively, a bureau de change can exchange foreign currencies for euros – you will need to have your ID card or passport to transact.

Note that when visiting remote regions of the island, it is a good idea to carry plenty of cash since it may be difficult to find an ATM, and businesses might not have the facility to accept credit cards. Look out for POS – Point of Sale; often a sign will indicate its presence or absence.

Telephone and Internet

Most foreign mobile phones work perfectly well on Crete. Roaming within the EU for all holders of EU SIMs is free within your monthly call and text allowance. North Americans and Australians should consider buying a local SIM card to save on roaming charges. Locked phones are easily unlocked in Greece.

The country code for Greece is 30. Local prefixes on Crete vary from place to place across the island. Both landlines and mobiles have ten digits, which must all be dialled in full, even in the same prefix zone. Most hotels, restaurants and cafés offer free Wi-Fi to guests.

Postal Services

Greece's **Hellenic Post (ELTA)** has main post offices in **Irakleio**, **Chania** and **Rethymno**, all of them open from 7:30am to 8:30pm Monday to Friday. Post offices in smaller towns and villages close earlier, at 2:30pm. Letter boxes are bright yellow.

TV, Radio and Newspapers

Three state-owned TV channels – ERT1, ERT2 and ERT3 – are run by the **Hellenic Radio and Television (ERT)**, and there are also countless private local channels. ERT also runs four national radio services (First, Second, Third Programmes and ERA Sport). Crete has many local radio stations that play a mix of pop, classical and traditional Cretan music. Reception may be weak in the mountains.

Hotel rooms usually have satellite TV, with international English-language channels such as **CNN**, **BBC** and **Euronews**.

Newsstands in the main cities and resorts stock major foreign-language newspapers, though they may be a day out-of-date.

Opening Hours

Cretan opening hours are erratic – use the times given in this book as a rough guide only. Most shops are open from 9am to 2pm Monday to Saturday. On Tuesdays, Thursdays and Fridays, they also open from 5:30–8:30pm. In tourist resorts, shops tend to open for longer in summer, sometimes until 10pm.

Banks are open from 8am to 2pm Monday to Thursday; and from 8am to 1:30pm Friday. Post offices open from 7:30am to 2:30pm Monday to Friday.

Major state-run archaeological sites and museums are open from 8am to 8pm in summer; many close on Mondays. Last entry is always 20 minutes before closure.

Monasteries, convents and churches are generally open during daylight hours but closed for 2 to 3 hours in the afternoon. Some smaller churches may even be locked; the key is usually held in the nearest village shop or café.

Banks, businesses and shops are closed on Greek public holidays: New Year's Day (1 Jan), Epiphany (6 Jan), Clean Monday, Independence Day (25 Mar), Good Friday, Easter Sunday, Easter Monday, Labour Day (1 May), Whit Monday, Assumption (15 Aug), Ohi Day (28 Oct), Christmas (25 Dec) and Boxing Day (26 Dec).

Time Difference

Greece is on Eastern European Time (EET), which is 2 hours ahead of Greenwich Mean Time (GMT) and 7 hours ahead of US Eastern Standard Time (EST). Summertime starts the last Sunday in March to the last Sunday in October.

Electrical Appliances

The electric current is 230 V (50Hz). Plugs have two round pins. UK visitors will need an adaptor for their appliances, and US visitors may need both a voltage converter and adaptor for their electronic devices.

Weather

Crete has a pleasant Mediterranean climate with plenty of sunshine. Summers are dry, with an average temperature of 26° C (79° F), but frequent maximums of 35° C (95° F). On the coast, gentle sea-breezes make the heat quite bearable.

In winter, the average temperature is 11° C (52° F), but at night it may drop below freezing, and Crete's mountains are often snowcapped from December through to April. Spring and autumn see average temperatures of around 16° C (61° F).

Summer (July–August) is the most popular time to visit, but those who prefer milder temperatures, fewer crowds and cheaper rates should consider May–June and September–October.

Shopping

Typical Cretan gifts to bring home include wine, *raki* or *tsikoudia*, olive oil, honey and handmade ceramics.

Where to Eat

Cretans tend to eat late: lunch can be any time between 1:30pm and 4pm, while dinner generally starts after 8:30pm and can go on until midnight.

A *taverna* is an informal and inexpensive eatery serving traditional dishes amid rustic decor. Plates may arrive at the table in a rather haphazard order; this is because there is less definition between courses, and diners often order dishes to share. A *psarotaverna* specializes in fish and seafood.

Other eateries include the *mezedopoleio*, serving small platters of *mezedes* (savoury snacks), along with carafes of barrel wine or *raki/tsikoudia*; and the *psistaria*, specializing in spit-roasted and char-grilled meats, especially sausages, chops and spit-roasts. A *gyradiko*, or a *souvlatzidiko* sell the popular *gyros* or *souvlaki* wrapped in pitta bread to take away.

Where to Stay

Crete offers everything from luxury resorts to backpackers' hostels. The biggest concentration of five-star resort hotels, complete with beaches and spas, is in Elounda, near Agios Nikolaos in eastern Crete. Boutique hotels in Chania and Rethymno may occupy Venetian-era buildings with period furnishings. Self-catering apartments offer greater freedom and flexibility. To escape the crowds, opt for a village guesthouse away from the coastal resorts, or to really savour rural life, stay at an agrotourism, a working farm offering accommodation and meals, generally prepared from its own home-grown produce.

Hotel rates depend on supply and demand, and prices peak in high season (Jul–Sep). Room prices almost always include breakfast. Major beach-side hotels are closed from November to April. Reliable accommodation sites include **Booking.com** and **hotelscombined.com** for hotels, **HostelWorld** for hostels and budget options, and **Airbnb** for apartments and rooms.

DIRECTORY

POSTAL SERVICES

Chania Main Post Office
MAP D2 ■ Peridou 10

Hellenic Post (ELTA)
w elta.gr

Irakleio Main Post Office
MAP T3 ■ Platia Daskalogianni 1

Rethymno Main Post Office
MAP F3 ■ Moatsou 19

TV, RADIO AND NEWSPAPERS

BBC
w bbc.com/news

CNN
w edition.cnn.com

Euronews
w euronews.com

Hellenic Radio and Television (ERT)
w int.ert.gr

WHERE TO STAY

Airbnb
w airbnb.com

Booking.com
w booking.com

HostelWorld
w hostelworld.com

HotelsCombined
w hotelscombined.com

Places to Stay

PRICE CATEGORIES
For a standard, double room per night (with breakfast if included), taxes and extra charges.
....
€ under €100   €€ €100–200   €€€ over €200

Luxury Resorts

Avra Imperial
MAP C2 ■ Kolymvari
■ 28240 84500 ■ www.
avraimperial.gr ■ €€€
Overlooking a sandy beach and a large outdoor pool lined with palms, Avra Imperial is one of western Crete's top resorts. It has 328 rooms and suites (some with private pools), a luxurious spa using Apivita beauty products, and a kids' club.

Blue Palace Resort and Spa
MAP N4 ■ Plaka, Elounda
■ 28410 65500 ■ www.
bluepalace.gr ■ €€€
The Blue Palace offers a superb mix of luxury suites, bungalows and villas with a spa, health centre, indoor and outdoor pools and tennis courts, plus a range of watersports.

Creta Maris Beach Resort
MAP M4 ■ Limin Chersonisos ■ 28970 27000 ■ www.maris.gr/creta ■ €€€
Located on the beach, the Creta Maris aims to provide a village atmosphere, with paths winding through lush grounds past a mix of bungalows, suites and rooms. The resort also offers a luxurious spa and activities such as Cretan dancing and cooking.

Daios Cove Luxury Resort
MAP N4 ■ Vathi, Agios Nikolaos ■ 28412 00488 ■ www.daioscovecrete. com ■ €€€
All rooms and suites have sea views at this family-friendly resort, and the villas have private pools. There is a beach offering watersports, plus tennis courts, a spa and a kids' club.

Domes of Elounda
MAP N4 ■ Elounda ■ 28410 43500 ■ www.domes ofelounda.com ■ €€€
Renowned for luxury and top service, this resort caters for both couples and families, with adult-only areas and a kids' club. It offers suites, residences and villas, a beach, a spa and four restaurants.

Elounda Mare Hotel
MAP N4 ■ S of Elounda ■ 28410 68200 ■ www.
eloundamare.com ■ €€€
The 96 units here include a mix of standard doubles and bungalows and suites with private pools. Facilities (some next door) include a nine-hole golf course, a spa and watersports.

Elounda Peninsula
MAP N4 ■ S of Elounda ■ 28410 68250 ■ www.
eloundapeninsula.com ■ €€€
On its own private peninsula, this hotel has

duplex suites, as well as larger villas with private pools. Facilities include a spa, tennis courts and a kids' club.

Grecotel Creta Palace
MAP F3 ■ Misiria ■ 28310 55181 ■ www.grecotel. com ■ €€€
Close to Rethymno, Creta Palace has 162 rooms in its main block, plus 200 bungalows and villas. It has several pools and a wide range of activities for children, as well as tennis courts and watersports.

Minoa Palace Resort & Spa
MAP C2 ■ Agia Marina ■ 28210 36500 ■ www.
minoapalace.gr ■ €€€
Close to Platanias and Chania, the Minoa Palace has a variety of rooms, suites and bungalows, some with private pools. The breakfasts are particularly good.

Minos Beach Art Hotel
MAP N4 ■ Agios Nikolaos ■ 28410 22345 ■ www.
minosbeach.com ■ €€€
This medium-sized complex of bungalows is set in tranquil gardens with views of the Gulf of Mirabello. A short stroll from the town centre, the hotel has its own sandy beaches and rocky inlets.

Out of the Blue Capsis Elite Resort
MAP K3 ■ Agia Pelagia, Irakleio ■ 28108 11112 ■ www.capsis.com ■ €€€
On a private headland, this five-star resort has its own beaches, a huge

swimming pool, a kids' club, restaurants and bars. Ideal for groups or families looking to stay in exclusive villas.

St Nicolas Bay Resort
MAP N4 ▪ Nisi Peninsula ▪ 28410 25041 ▪ www.stnicolasbay.gr ▪ €€€
This multi award-winning complex, just outside Agios Nikolaos, has well-equipped rooms, suites and villas, and three restaurants. Watersports are also offered.

Boutique Hotels

Alcanea Boutique Hotel
MAP A5 ▪ Angelou 2, Chania ▪ 28210 75370 ▪ Closed in winter ▪ www.ariahotels.gr ▪ €€
Situated in the harbour, above the Naval Museum, this hotel occupies the former office of Cretan revolutionary hero Eleftherios Venizelos. Rooms are painted in soothing pastels and have views of the harbour and sea.

Avli Lounge Suites
MAP Q2 ▪ Rethymno ▪ 28310 58250 ▪ Open all year ▪ www.avli.gr ▪ €€
Centrally located, Avli has 12 comfortable suites, some with a Jacuzzi or terrace, spread over three Venetian-era buildings. Breakfast is served in the courtyard restaurant, along with a less formal *mezedopoleio*, Raki Ba Raki.

Casa Leone
MAP D2 ▪ Parodos Theotokopoulou 18, Chania ▪ 28210 76762 ▪ www.casa-leone.com ▪ €€€
The "House of the Lion" has been meticulously

restored, with period details such as Venetian mirrors and antique and reproduction furniture.

Casa Vitae
MAP Q2 ▪ Neophytou Patelarou 3, Rethymno ▪ 28310 35058 ▪ www.casa-vitae.gr ▪ €€
In a Venetian-era building with a courtyard (where breakfast is served), these doubles or suites have exposed stone walls, tiled floors and wooden-beamed ceilings. Some also have a four-poster bed, a balcony or a Jacuzzi bath.

Lato
MAP T1 ▪ Epimenidou 15, Irakleio ▪ 2810 228103 ▪ www.lato.gr ▪ €€
This trendy-modern boutique hotel has many units, which have great views over the Venetian port. The breakfast is decent and there is a good but pricey rooftop restaurant. The hotel has valet parking, too.

Mythos Suites
MAP F3 ▪ C12 Plateia Karaoli, Rethymno ▪ 28310 53917 ▪ www.mythos-crete.gr ▪ €€
This hotel occupies two 16th-century Venetian buildings that have been knocked together. It is centred on a courtyard with a pool; ground floor rooms have verandas, while rooms on the upper floors have wooden balconies.

Palazzino di Corina
MAP Q1 ▪ Damvergi 7–9, Rethymno ▪ 28310 21205/06 ▪ www.corina.gr ▪ €€
This lovingly restored Venetian mansion in

the old town has 29 small rooms and suites, some with Jacuzzi baths and four-poster beds. There is a plunge-pool in the charming patio, a lively street-side bar and an excellent restaurant.

Pandora Suites
MAP D2 ▪ Lithinon 29, Chania ▪ 28210 43588 ▪ www.pandora-hotel.com ▪ €€
This is a stylish collection of two- and four-person suites, some facing an inner courtyard, others looking out to sea. All have balconies and tall, shuttered windows.

Ambassador's Residence
MAP D2 ▪ Akti Tompazi 29–30, Chania ▪ 28216 00855 ▪ www.ambassadorsresidence chania.com ▪ €€€
In a 19th-century building overlooking the harbour, these nine suites are contemporary and stylish. Each is inspired by a different material: wood, ceramic or glass. Some have a terrace or a Jacuzzi.

Casa Delfino
MAP D2 ▪ Theofanous 9, Chania ▪ 28210 93098 ▪ www.casadelfino.com ▪ €€€
This early 19th-century, Genoese-built mansion, Chania's most exclusive address, has been luxuriously restored by a descendant of the original Delfino family. All 24 suites are unique, having a *hamam* or vaulted ceiling, balcony or even a roof terrace.

Kapsaliana Village Hotel

MAP G4 ■ Kapsaliana, near Arkadi ■ 28310 83400 ■ www.kapsaliana village.gr ■ €€€
Twelve typically Cretan and Venetian houses in this village have been converted into 17 guesthouses, each combining original features with modern comforts such as Wi-Fi and DVD players. The complex also has a pool, a restaurant and an old olive press.

La Maison Ottomane

MAP A5 ■ Parodos Kanevarou 32, Chania ■ 28210 08796 ■ www. lamaisonottomane.com ■ €€€
This romantic hideaway has just three elegant rooms, furnished with period antiques and artworks, plus modern luxuries such as in-room espresso machines and tablet computers. Breakfast and drinks are served in a pretty, peaceful courtyard.

Villa Andromeda

MAP D2 ■ Elfetheriou Venizelou 150, Chania ■ 28210 28300 ■ Closed Nov–Mar ■ www. villandromeda.gr ■ €€€
This converted Neo-Classical mansion has eight wood-floored suites, many with balconies, painted ceilings in the communal areas and a landscaped pool.

Beach Hotels

Alianthos Garden Hotel

MAP F4 ■ Plakias ■ 28320 31280 ■ www.hotel alianthos.com ■ €€
A block inland from one of Crete's nicest beaches, this family-run hotel is the best in Plakias. It has a children's pool, freshwater pool and poolside bar, plus a market and a restaurant.

Ammos Hotel

MAP C2 ■ Agioi Apostoli ■ 28210 33003 ■ www.ammoshotel.com ■ Closed Dec–Mar ■ €€
Behind a sandy beach, this stylish hotel west of Chania is filled with contemporary, hip design and artworks. It has 33 mostly sea-view studios or suites, plus an all-day restaurant, pool, massage room, gym and playroom.

Corinna Mare

MAP D2 ■ Kalamaki, Nea Kydonia ■ 28210 31767 ■ www.corinna.gr ■ €€
On a small peninsula west of Chania, facing Theodorou islet, this peaceful hotel has 49 rooms, suites and apartments. There is a restaurant, two outdoor pools, sauna and gym, plus baby-sitting and massage on request.

Iberostar Creta Panorama & Mare

MAP G3 ■ Panormos ■ 28340 51502 ■ www.iberostar.com ■ €€
Four outdoor pools, a heated indoor pool, six tennis courts, sauna and water sports, make this huge beach resort one of the best in Crete for an active holiday. Accommodation is in suites or bungalows.

Irini Mare

MAP G5 ■ Main beach, Agia Galini ■ 28320 91051 ■ www.irinimare.com ■ €€
This is a small, family-run hotel in a tranquil spot. There is a pool and a kids' playground, and most rooms or suites have balconies with a sea view. Great buffet breakfasts and half-board rates.

Kalyves Beach Hotel

MAP E2 ■ Kalyves ■ 28250 31285 ■ www.kalyvesbeach.com ■ €€
Situated between two sandy beaches on Souda Bay, this hotel overlooks the Xydas river and has 150 rooms in two wings, each with a pool. There is an attractive riverside terrace restaurant and easy beach access.

Porto Loutro Hotel

MAP D4 ■ Loutro, Anopoli ■ 28250 91433 ■ No credit cards ■ www.hotelportoloutro.com ■ €€
This attractive hotel just above the shoreline has 36 rooms (plus four self-catering studios) in two buildings in separate parts of this village, set among palm trees and bougainvillea. No children under seven are allowed.

Sitia Bay Hotel

MAP Q4 ■ Patriarhou Vartholomeou 27/Tritis Septemvriou 8, Siteia ■ 28430 24800 ■ www.sitiabay.com ■ €€
This hotel has 19 studios and suites with kitchens and balconies with sea views. Amenities include free Wi-Fi and a rooftop terrace. There is also a small gym, a sauna and a chlorine-free pool with hydro-massage.

Pilot Beach Resort

MAP E3 ■ Georgioupolis ■ 28250 61002 ■ www.pilot-beach.gr ■ €€€
This resort has well-appointed bungalows and suites, extensive sports

facilities, pools and plenty of fun activities for kids. Enjoy food and nightlife in the resort's four restaurants and three bars.

Village Guesthouses

Aspros Potamos Cottages

MAP P5 ▪ Aspros Potamos, Makrygialos, Ierapetra ▪ 28430 51694 ▪ No air conditioning ▪ www.asprospotamos.com ▪ €

These utterly lovely shepherds' cottages, with stone floors, wooden ceilings and fireplace nooks, are set among groves of pine, olive and carob trees. Although accommodation is self-catering, breakfast is available on request. There is a tiny swimming pool on site.

The Blue House

MAP D4 ▪ Loutro ▪ 28250 91127 ▪ www.thebluehouse.gr ▪ €

Balconies overlook the bay and the slopes of the White Mountains at this amiable guesthouse. It is particularly handy as an overnight stop on the way to or from Agia Roumeli and the Samaria Gorge.

Corali Studios and Portobello Apartments

MAP N4 ▪ Akti Posidonos, Elounda ▪ 28410 41712 ▪ www.coralistudios.com ▪ €

A short walk from the town centre, these family-run studios and apartments have their own pool and gardens. They also offer easy access to the town beach and watersports.

Hotel Marina

MAP H4 ▪ Main street, Anogeia ▪ 28340 31817 ▪ €

This modern village inn has 16 apartments, including four larger ones for families. Each apartment has a kitchen, a TV, a balcony with a view of the Psiloritis range and a fireplace.

Keramos Studios

MAP J5 ▪ Zaros ▪ 28940 31352 ▪ www.studiokeramos-zaros.gr ▪ €

Famous for its breakfasts, which include homemade pies and cheeses, this welcoming, family-run B&B offers 18 basic but comfortable rooms with balconies, a lounge with a fireplace, and visits to the family farm.

Terramara Rooms

MAP B2 ▪ Plakalon ▪ 69406 94904 ▪ No credit cards ▪ www.terramaracrete.com ▪ €

On a hill surrounded by olive groves, Terramara offers spectacular views of the Gulf of Kissamos. Facilities include a pool, barbecue area, bar and laundry service. There are four inter-connected rooms that are ideal for families.

Arolithos

MAP J4 ▪ Arolithos, Servili, Tylissos ▪ 2810 821050 ▪ www.arolithos.com ▪ €€

At this complex of stone houses, you can take part in an array of traditional crafts – from pottery and icon painting, to basket weaving and embroidery. Traditional music and dance are performed nightly in the affiliated restaurant.

Monastery Estate Guesthouse

MAP C4 ▪ 4 km above Moni, Sougia ▪ 6944 711 277 ▪ www.monasteryestate.com ▪ €€

In the mountains near Sougia, this complex of 19th-century buildings has been turned into five luxurious two-room apartments. Cavernous and whitewashed, each has a kitchen and terrace.

Nakou Village

MAP N6 ▪ Koutsounari, 9 km (6 miles) from Ierapetra ▪ 28420 61815 ▪ Some air conditioning ▪ www.nakoutradition.gr ▪ €€

Stay in a fully modernized stone cottage or studio at this hillside holiday village. All have verandas or gardens, and there is a pool and taverna next door. Minimum stay is a week.

Rodanthi Guesthouse

MAP E3 ▪ Kastello Apokoronou ▪ 28250 96270 ▪ www.rodanthihotel.gr ▪ €€

In a beautiful hillside village between Chania and Rethymno, this farmhouse stands in a walled garden with a large pool and barbecue. Its four rooms have period furniture, and there is a kitchen where guests can make their own breakfast.

Villa Archanes

MAP K4 ▪ Ano Archanes ▪ 6973 632 204 ▪ www.villaarchanes.gr ▪ €€

Providing a fine base for winery visits, this stone mansion from 1890 lies in vineyard country, south of Irakleio. It has six apartments (sleeping two–five), an outdoor pool and barbecue, and a gym, plus massage on request.

For a key to hotel price categories see p128

Villa Kerasia

MAP J4 ▪ Vlachiana ▪ 2810 791021 ▪ www.villa-kerasia.gr ▪ €€
Some 15 km (9 miles) inland from Irakleio, with hiking trails nearby, this welcoming villa is set in a garden with a pool. It offers seven rooms, some with four-poster beds. The restaurant serves breakfast and dinner.

Self-Catering Apartments

Anna View Apartments

MAP F4 ▪ Myrthios village ▪ 697 3324 775 ▪ Open all year ▪ www.annaview.com ▪ €
Constructed in wood and stone, these family-run apartments have spectacular views over Plakias Bay. Beautifully furnished, they come with a kitchenette, satellite TV and Wi-Fi.

Bay View Apartments

MAP Q4 ▪ Petras, Siteia ▪ 28430 24333 ▪ No credit cards ▪ No air conditioning ▪ Winter rentals by the month ▪ www.bayview-apartments.gr ▪ €
Located near the main Siteia beach, these seven apartments (three one-bedroom, four two-bedrooms) have pleasant furnishings and superb views over the bay and the town.

Lefka Apartments

MAP D2 ▪ Odos Omirou, Yermaniko Pouli, Chania ▪ 28210 73310 ▪ www.lefka-apartments.gr ▪ €
Just outside Chania, close to some lovely beaches, the Lefka apartment complex has a garden with a free-form pool and snack bar. The eight studios and eight apartments (sleeping two–four) are basic but come with kitchens and balconies.

Metohi Vaï Village

MAP R4 ▪ S of Vaï Beach ▪ 28430 61071 ▪ www.4ty.gr/merchant/12313/en/METOHIVAI ▪ €
The only accommodation option this close to the Vaï palm beach. The seven apartments here occupy old shepherds' shelters converted into comfortable apartments with kitchens and soaring arches. Some have working fireplaces.

Paul-Eva Apartments

MAP M4 ▪ Sokratous 15, Koutouloufari, Chersonisos ▪ 28970 23358 ▪ €
Extremely affordable apartments, only 1 km (half a mile) from the beach, each with private balconies and basic amenities, plus a shared pool.

Stella's Traditional Apartments-Studios

MAP R5 ▪ Kato Zakros village ▪ 28430 23739 ▪ www.stelapts.com ▪ €
Stella's offers stone-built, traditionally furnished studios (fits 2–4) or larger apartments in the Terra Minoika section, set amid lush landscaping with hammocks on the terrace. There is fresh spring water on tap, and a communal clothes washing machine.

Villa Anna Apartments

MAP B4 ▪ Paleochora ▪ 2810 346428 ▪ No credit cards ▪ www.villaanna-paleochora.com ▪ €
Set amid vast gardens, this 8-unit complex is located on a quiet side street close to the sandy beach. All apartments have a living room, kitchen and veranda, plus one or two bedrooms. There is also a children's play area.

Aptera Hotel

MAP D2 ▪ Aptera, Apokoronou, Chania ▪ 28250 31440 ▪ No credit cards ▪ Breakfast available on extra charge ▪ www.aptera-lodge.com ▪ €€
These well-equipped studio and one or two bedroom apartments near the ancient Aptera overlook Souda Bay and the White Mountains.

Elounda Water Park Residence

MAP N4 ▪ Odos Emmanouil Pouli, Schisma, Elounda ▪ 28410 41823 ▪ www.eloundaresidence.gr ▪ €€
Set in lush gardens a 15-minute walk south of central Elounda, this holiday complex has a water park and an all-inclusive meal plan that complements its two- to four-person apartments. Other facilities include a saltwater pool, a kids' club and a gym.

Natalia's Houses

MAP E3 ▪ Douliana village ▪ 28250 23356 ▪ www.nataliashouses.gr ▪ €€
Charming Natalia's has four self-catering suites (two with fireplaces) in restored stone buildings, which can accommodate three to six people. There is a shop, a pool, a bar and a barbecue area. Guests can enjoy views of the White Mountains from here.

White River Cottages

MAP P5 ▪ Aspros Potamos, Makrygialos ▪ 28430 51120 ▪ www.whiterivercottages.com ▪ €€
This romantic boho-chic retreat surrounded by olive

groves comprises 15 self-catering cottages (capacity two–four) built into the rock, with stone floors and wooden ceilings. The large, deep focal pool has gazebos for shade and reliable Wi-Fi signal.

Yiannis Retreat
MAP R5 ▪ Kato Zakros, 500 m (1,640 ft) inland ▪ 28430 25726 ▪ www.katozakros-rooms.com ▪ €€
In a lush garden with palms, hammocks and a barbecue area, these five studios have exposed stone walls, terracotta floors, wooden-beamed ceilings, traditional wooden furniture and kitchenettes. Mountain bikes are available for free.

Agrotourism

Argoulias
MAP M4 ▪ Tzermiado ▪ 28440 22754 ▪ www.argoulias.gr ▪ €
Comprising 11 stone-built apartments and a rustic restaurant serving breakfast, Argoulias also arranges hiking trips and local farm visits on the Lasithi Plateau.

Lasinthos Eco Park
MAP M5 ▪ Agios Georgios ▪ 28440 89101 ▪ www.lasinthos.gr ▪ €
On the Lasithi Plateau, this eco-park has 20 apartments and a restaurant. It is ideal for families with children. Activities on offer include craft workshops and feeding the animals – goats, sheep, cows, horses, chickens and ducks.

Milia Mountain Retreat
MAP B3 ▪ Milia, Vlatos ▪ 28210 46774 ▪ www.milia.gr ▪ €
Set in a wooded valley, accessed via a winding

rough track, Milia offers 13 rooms in restored stone cottages, heated by wood-burning stoves, with mountain spring water and solar-panel electricity. Milia's taverna serves several local delicacies.

Mourtzanakis Residence
MAP K3 ▪ Achlada ▪ 2810 812096 ▪ www.ecotourismgreece.com ▪ €
In the hills behind Agia Pelagia, this welcoming ecotourism centre offers modern purpose-built apartments, two small pools (kids/adults) and optional communal meals. It also offers a special "olive harvest" package.

Sarris House
MAP C2 ▪ Xirokampi, inland from Maleme ▪ 28210 73944 ▪ www.sarris-house.gr ▪ €
Set in a garden with a pool, this renovated farmhouse can accommodate nine guests. It grows its own organic fruit and vegetables. Activities range from cooking lessons and pottery to horse riding. During August/September, guests can help with the grape harvest.

Thalori Traditional Village
MAP K6 ▪ Kapetaniana ▪ 28930 41762 ▪ www.thalori.com ▪ €
In the mountains above the south coast, this rural retreat offers 20 studios and cottages with exposed stone walls and wooden-beamed ceilings, as well as a taverna that uses local produce. Thalori makes a fine base for hiking and visiting nearby beaches.

Dalabelos
MAP G3 ▪ Angeliana ▪ 28340 22155 ▪ www.dalabelos.gr ▪ €€
With vineyards and orchards, along with goats, chickens and a donkey, this farm has ten stone-built one-bedroom apartments, a courtyard restaurant with its own wine, and a pool. Guests are welcome to help on the farm.

Eleonas
MAP H5 ▪ Zaros ▪ 28940 31238 ▪ www.eleonas.gr ▪ €€
A farm with olive groves, Eleonas has 20 stone cottages, an outdoor pool, bikes for hire and an excellent taverna (see p97) that serves dishes made from local produce. It is set in a lovely rural location, with a gorge and a lake accessible via marked hiking paths.

Enagron
MAP H4 ▪ Axos Mylopotamou ▪ 28340 61611 ▪ www.enagron.gr ▪ €€
Located amid lush vineyards and olive groves, this ecotourism complex has 32 purpose-built, stone-and-wood apartments (studios–three rooms), a taverna, a café, a spa and an outdoor pool. Activities include bread-making and wine tasting.

Vamos
MAP E3 ▪ Vamos, Apokoronou ▪ 28250 22190 ▪ www.vamosvillage.gr ▪ €€
In an abandoned former village, these stone villas and cottages have been lovingly restored; family-sized ones also have pools. Vamos arranges cookery lessons, olive-mill and winery visits, and hiking.

For a key to hotel price categories see p128

Index

Acknowledgments

Author
Robin Gauldie is a freelance travel writer and photographer based in the UK

Additional Contributor
Jane Foster

Publishing Director Georgina Dee

Publisher Vivien Antwi

Design Director Phil Ormerod

Editorial Ankita Awasthi Tröger, Alice Fewery, Rachel Fox, Maresa Manara, Sands Publishing Solutions, Sally Schafer, Anupama Shukla

Design Bhavika Mathur, Marisa Renzullo

Cover Design Richard Czapnik

Commissioned Photography Robin Gauldie, Rough Guides / Geoff Garvey, Tony Souter

Picture Research Subhadeep Biswas, Taiyaba Khatoon, Sumita Khatwani, Ellen Root, Rituraj Singh

Cartography Martin Darlison, Suresh Kumar, James Macdonald, Zafar-ul-Islam Khan

Crete map derived from East View Cartographic database, www.cartographic.com

DTP Jason Little

Production Igrain Roberts

Factchecker Marc Dubin

Proofreader Laura Walker

Indexer Helen Peters

VladimirSklyarov 68b, 112-3.

Kaaren's, Elounda: 118crb.

Municipality of Chania: 49cla.

Ourios Ceramics: 106c.

Rex Shutterstock: Stefanos Rapanis /EPA 82clb.

Robert Harding Picture Library: Stuart Black 15cr; Maria Breuer 59cra.

Scalani Hills Boutari Winery & Residences: 95cl.

SuperStock: age fotostock /Peter Erik Forsberg 96t, /Phil Robinson 78tl; Albatross 46clb; Album /Oronoz 54c; BEW Authors / BE&W 44b; Katja Kreder / imageBROKER 119bl; Juniors 66tl.

Veneto, Rethymno: 73clb.

Cover

Front and spine: **Alamy Stock Photo:** robertharding

Back: **123RF.com:** Milan Gonda

Pull Out Map Cover

Alamy Stock Photo: robertharding

All other images © Dorling Kindersley

For further information see:
www.dkimages.com

Penguin
Random
House

Printed and bound in China

First American Edition 2005
Published in the United States by
DK Publishing, 345 Hudson Street,
New York, New York 10014

Copyright 2003, 2018 © Dorling
Kindersley Limited

A Penguin Random House Company

18 19 20 21 10 9 8 7 6 5 4 3 2 1

Reprinted with revisions 2005, 2009, 2011, 2013, 2015, 2018

Published in Great Britain by Dorling Kindersley Limited.

A catalog record for this book is available from the Library of Congress.

ISSN 1479-344X
ISBN 978 1 4654 6549 8

MIX
Paper from
responsible sources
FSC
www.fsc.org   FSC™ C018179

SPECIAL EDITIONS OF DK TRAVEL GUIDES

DK Travel Guides can be purchased in bulk quantities at discounted prices for use in promotions or as premiums. We are also able to offer special editions and personalized jackets, corporate imprints, and excerpts from all of our books, tailored specifically to meet your own needs.

To find out more, please contact:

in the US
specialsales@dk.com

in the UK
travelguides@uk.dk.com

in Canada
specialmarkets@dk.com

in Australia
**penguincorporatesales@
penguinrandomhouse.com.au**

*As a guide to abbreviations in visitor information blocks: **Adm** = admission charge; **DA** = disabled access; **D** = dinner; **L** = lunch.*

Phrase Book

In an Emergency

English	Greek	Pronunciation
Help!	Voítheia!	vo-ee-theea!
Stop!	Stamatíste!	sta-ma-tee-steh!
Call a doctor!	Fonáxte éna giatró!	fo-nak-steh e-na ya-tro!
Call an ambulance/ the police/ fire brigade!	Kaléste to asthenofóro/ tin astynomía/tin pyrosvestikí!	ka-le-steh to as-the-no-fo-ro/ teen a-sti-no-the mia/teen pee-ro-zve-stee-kee!
Where is the nearest telephone/ hospital/ pharmacy?	Poú eínai to plisiéstero tiléfono/ nosokomeío/ farmakeío?	poo ee-ne to plee-see-e-ste-ro tee-le-pho-no/ no-so-ko-mee-o/ far-ma-kee-o?

Communication Essentials

English	Greek	Pronunciation
Yes	Nai	neh
No	Ochi	o-chee
Please	Parakaló	pa-ra-ka-lo
Thank you	Efcharistó	ef-cha-ree-sto
You are welcome	Parakaló	pa-ra-ka-lo
OK/alright	Entáxei	en-dak-zee
Excuse me	Me synchoreíte	me seen-cho-ree-teh
Hello	Geiá sas	yeea sas
Goodbye	Antío	an-dee-o
Good morning	Kaliméra	ka-lee-me-ra
Good night	Kalin'ychta	ka-lee-neech-ta
Morning	Proí	pro-ee
Afternoon	Apógevma	a-po-yev-ma
Evening	Vrádi	vrath-i
This morning	Símera to proí	see-me-ra to pro-ee
Yesterday	Chthés	chthes
Today	Símera	see-me-ra
Tomorrow	Avrio	av-ree-o
Here	Edó	ed-o
There	Ekeí	e-kee
What?	Tí?	tee?
Why?	Giatí?	ya-tee?
Where?	Poú?	poo?
How?	Pós?	pos?
Wait!	Perímene!	pe-ree-me-neh!
How are you?	Tí káneis?	tee ka-nees?
Very well, thank you.	Poly kalá, efcharistó.	po-lee ka-la, ef-cha-ree-sto.
How do you do?	Pós eíste?	pos ees-te?
Pleased to meet you.	Chaíro pol'y.	che-ro po-lee.
What is your name?	Pós légeste?	pos le-ye-ste?
Where is/are…?	Poú eínai…?	poo ee-neá?
How far is it to…?	Póso apéchei…?	po-so a-pe-chee?
How do I get to..?	Pós mporó na páo…?	pos bo-ro-na pa-o…?
Do you speak English?	Miláte Angliká?	mee-la-te an-glee-ka?
I understand.	Katalavaíno.	ka-ta-la-ve-no.
I don't understand	Den katalavaíno.	then ka-ta-la-ve-no.
Could you speak slowly?	Miláte lígo pio argá parakaló?	mee-la-te lee-go pyo ar-ga pa-ra-ka-lo?
I'm sorry.	Me synchoreíte.	me seen-cho-ree teh.
Does anyone have a key?	Echei kanénas kleidí?	e-chee ka-ne-nas klee-dee?

Useful Words

English	Greek	Pronunciation
big	Megálo	me-ga-lo
small	Mikró	mi-kro
hot	Zestó	zes-to
cold	Kr'yo	kree-o
good	Kaló	ka-lo
bad	Kakó	ka-ko
enough	Arketá	ar-ke-ta
well	Kalá	ka-la
open	Anoichtá	a-neech-ta
closed	Kleistá	klee-sta
left	Aristerá	a-ree-ste-ra
right	Dexiá	dek-see-a
straight on	Eftheía	ef-thee-a
between	Anámesa / Metax'y	a-na-me-sa/ me-tak-see
on the corner of…	Sti gonía tou…	stee go-nee-a too kon-da
near	Kontá	kon-da
far	Makriá	ma-kree-a
up	Epáno	e-pa-no
down	Káto	ka-to
early	Norís	no-rees
late	Argá	ar-ga
entrance	I eísodos	ee ee-so-thos
exit	I éxodos	ee e-kso-dos
toilet occupied/ engaged	Oi toualétes / Kateiliméni	ee-too-a-le-tes ka-tee-lee-me-nee
unoccupied	Eléftheri	e-lef-the-ree
free/no charge	Doreán	tho-re-an
in/out	Mésa/Exo	me-sa/ek-so

Making a Telephone Call

English	Greek	Pronunciation
Where is the nearest public telephone?	Poú vrísketai o plisiésteros tilefonikós thálamos?	poo vrees-ke-teh o plee-see-e-ste-ros tee-le-fo-ni-kos tha-la-mos?
I would like to place a long-distance call.	Tha íthela na káno éna yperastikó tilefónima.	tha ee-the-la na ka-no e-na ee-pe-ra-sti-ko tee-le-fo-nee-ma.
I would like to reverse the charges.	Tha íthela na chreóso to tilefónima ston paralípti.	tha ee-the-la na chre-o-so to tee-le-fo-nee-ma ston pa-ra-lep-tee.
I will try again later.	Tha xanatilefoníso argótera.	tha ksa-na-tee-le-fo-ni-so ar-go-te-ra.
Can I leave a message?	Mporeíte na tou afísete éna mínyma?	bo-ree-te na too a-fee-se-teh e-na mee-nee-ma?
Could you speak up a little please?	Miláte dynatótera, parakaló?	mee-la-teh dee-na-to-te -ra, pa-ra-ka-lo?
Hold on.	Períménete.	pe-ri-me-ne-teh.
local call	Topikó tilefónima	to-pi-ko tee-le-fo-nee-ma
OTE telephone office	O OTE /To tilefoneío	o O-TE /To tee-le-fo-nee-o
phone box/kiosk	O tilefonikós thálamos	o tee-le-fo-ni-kos tha-la-mos
phone card	I tilekárta	tee-le-kar-ta

Shopping

English	Greek	Pronunciation
How much does this cost?	Póso kánei?	po-so ka-nee?
I would like…	Tha íthela…	tha ee-the-la…
Do you have…?	Echete…?	e-che-tehá?
I am just looking.	Aplós koitáo.	a-plos kee-ta-o.
Do you take travellers' cheques/ travellers' cheques?	Décheste pistotikés kártes/ travellers' cheques?	the-ches-teh pee-sto-tee-kes kar-tes/ travellers cheques/?
What time do you open/close?	Póte anoígete/ kleínete?	po-teh a-nee-ye-teh/ klee-ne-teh?
Can you ship this overseas?	Mporeíte na to steílete sto exoterikó?	bo-ree-teh na to stee-le-teh sto e-xo-te-ree ko?
This one.	Aftó edó.	af-to e-do.
That one.	Ekeíno.	e-kee-no.
expensive	Akrivó	a-kree-vo
cheap	Fthinó	fthee-no
size	To mégethos	to me-ge-thos

white	Lefkó	lef-ko
black	Mávro	mav-ro
red	Kókkino	ko-kee-no
yellow	Kítrino	kee-tree-no
green	Prásino ·	pra-see-no
blue	Mple	bleh

Types of Shop

antique shop	Magazí me antíkes	ma-ga-zee me an-dee-kes
bakery	O foúrnos	o foor-nos
bank	I trápeza	ee tra-pe-za
bazaar	To pazári	to pa-za-ree
bookshop	To vivliopoleío	to vee-vlee-o-po-lee-o
butcher	To kreopoleío	to kre-o-po-lee-o
cake shop	To zacharoplasteío	to za-cha-ro-pla-stee-o
cheese shop	Magazí me allantiká	ma-ga-zee me a-lan-dee-ka
department store	Polykatástima	Po-lee-ka-ta-stee-ma
fishmarket	To ichthyopoleío/ psarádiko	to eech-thee-o-po-lee-o /psa-rá-dee-ko
greengrocer	To manáviko	to ma-na-vee-ko
hairdresser	To kommotírio	to ko-mo-tee-ree-o
kiosk	To períptero	to pe-reep-te-ro
leather shop	Magazí me dermátina eíd	ma-ga-zee me ther-ma-tee-na ee-thee
street market	I laïkí agorá	ee la-ee-kee a-go-ra
newsagent	O efimeridopólis	O e-fee-me-ree-tho-po-lees
pharmacy	To farmakeío	to far-ma-kee-o
post office	To tachydromeío	to ta-chee-thro-mee-o
shoe shop	Katástima me podimáton	ka-ta-stee-ma ee-po-dee-ma-ton
souvenir shop	Magazí me "souvenir"	ma-ga-zee meh "souvenir"
supermarket	"Supermarket" / Yperagorá	"Supermarket" / ee-per-a-go-ra
tobacconist	Eidi kapnoú	Ee-thee kap-nees
travel agent	To taxeidiotikó grafeío	to tak-see-thy-o-tee-ko gra-fee-o

Sightseeing

tourist information	O EOT	o E-OT
tourist police	I touristikí astynomía	ee too-rees-tee-kee a-stee-no-mee-a
archaeological	archaiologikós	ar-che-o-lo-yee-kos
art gallery	I gkalerí	ee ga-le-ree
beach	I paralía	ee pa-ra-lee-a
Byzantine	vyzantinós	vee-zan-dee-nos
castle	To kástro	to ka-stro
cathedral	I mitrópoli	ee mee-tro-po-lee
cave	To spílaio	to spee-le-o
church	I ekklisía	ee e-klee-see-a
folk art	laïkí téchni	la-ee-kee tech-nee
fountain	To syntriváni	to seen-dree-va-nee
garden	O kípos	o kee-pos
gorge	To farángi	to fa-ran-gee
grave of….	O táfos tou…	o ta-fos too
hill	O lófos	o lo-fos
historical	istorikós	ee-sto-ree-kos
island	To nisí	to nee-see
lake	I límni	ee leem-nee
library	I vivliothíki	ee veev-lee-o-thee-kee
mansion	I épavlis	ee e-pav-lees
monastery	moní	mo-ni
mountain	To vounó	to voo-no
municipal	dimotikós	thee-mo-tee-kos
museum	To mouseío	to moo-see-o
national	ethnikós	eth-nee-kos
park	To párko	to par-ko
river	To potámi	to po-ta-mee

road	O drómos	o thro-mos
saint	ágios/ágioi agía/agíes	a-yee-os/a-yee-ee/a-yee-a/ a-yee-es
spring	I pigí	ee pee-yee
square	I plateía	ee pla-tee-a
stadium	To stádio	to sta-thee-o
statue	To ágalma	to a-gal-ma
theatre	To théatro	to the-a-tro
town hall	To dimarcheío	to thee-mar-chee-o
closed on public holidays	kleistó tis argíes	klee-sto tees aryee-es

Transport

When does the … leave?	Póte févgei to…?	po-teh fev-yee to…?
Where is the bus stop?	Poú eínai i stási tou leoforeíou?	poo ee-neh ee sta-see too le-o-fo-ree-oo…?
Is there a bus to?	Ypárchei leoforeío gia…?	ee-par-chee le-o-fo-ree-o yia…?
ticket office	Ekdotíria eisitiríon	Ek-tho-tee-reea ee-see-tee-ree-on
return ticket	Eisitírio me epistrofí	ee-see-tee-ree-o meh e-pee-stro-fee
single journey	Apló eisitírio	a-plo ee-see-tee-reeo
bus station	O stathmós leoforeíon	o stath-mos leo-fo-ree-on
bus ticket	Eisitírio leoforeíou	ee-see-tee-ree-o leo-fo-ree-oo
trolley bus	To trólley	to tro-le-ee
port	To limáni	to lee-ma-nee
train/metro	To tréno	to tre-no
railway station	sidirodromikós stathmós	see-thee-ro-thro-mee-kos stath-mos
moped	To motopodílato / To michanáki	to mo-to-po-thee-la-to/to mee-cha-na-kee
bicycle	To podílato	to po-thee-la-to
taxi	To taxí	to tak-see
airport	To aeródromio	to a-e-ro-thro-mee-o
ferry	To "ferry-boat"	to fe-ree-bot
hydrofoil	To delfíni / To ydroptérygo	to del-fee-nee /To ee-throp-te-ree-go
catamaran for hire	To katamarán Enoikiázontai	to catamaran e-nee-kya-zon-deh

Staying in a Hotel

Do you have a vacant room?	Echete domátia?	e-che-teh tho-ma-tee-a?
I have a reservation.	Echo kánei krátisi.	e-cho ka-nee kra-tee-see.
double room with double bed	Díklino me dipló kreváti	thee-klee-no meh thee-plo kre-va-tee
twin room	Díklino me dipló kreváti	thee-klee-no meh mo-na kre-vat-ya
single room	Monóklino	mo-no-klee-no
room with a bath	Domátio me mpánio	tho-ma-tee-o meh ban-yo
shower	To douz	To dooz
porter	O portiéris	o por-tye-rees
key	To kleidí	to klee-dee
room with a sea view/balcony	Domátio me théa sti thálassa/ mpalkóni	tho-ma-tee-o meh the-a stee tha-la-sa/bal-ko-nee
Does the price include breakfast?	To proïnó symperilamvánetai stin timí?	to pro-ee-no seem-be-ree-lam-va-ne-teh steen tee-mee?

Eating Out

| Have you got a table? | Echete trapézi? | e-che-te tra-pe-zee? |

English	Greek	Pronunciation
I want to reserve a table.	Thélo na kratíso éna trapézi.	the-lo na kra-tee-so e-na tra-pe-zee.
The bill, please.	Ton logariazmó	ton lo-gar-yas-mo pa-ra-ka-ló, parakaló.
I am a vegetarian.	Eímai chortofágos.	ee-meh chor-to-fa-gos.
What is fresh today?	Tí frésko échete símera?	tee fres-ko e-che-teh see-me-ra?
waiter/waitress	K'yrie/Garson"/ Kyría	Kee-ree-eh/Gar-son/Kee-ree-a
menu	O katálogos	o ka-ta-lo-gos
cover charge	To "couvert"	to koo-ver
wine list	O katálogos me ta oinopo-vmatódi	o ka-ta-lo-gos meh ta ee-no-pnev-ma-to-thee
glass	To potíri	to po-tee-ree
bottle	To mpoukáli	to bou-ka-lee
knife	To machaíri	to ma-che-ree
fork	To pirouíni	to pee-roo-nee
spoon	To koutáli	to koo-ta-lee
breakfast	To proïnó	to pro-ee-no
lunch	To mesimerianó	to me-see-mer-ya-no
dinner	To deípno	to theep-no
main course	To kyrios gévma	to kee-ree-os yev-ma
starter/first course	Ta orektiká	ta o-rek-tee-ka
dessert	To glykó	to ylee-ko
dish of the day	To piáto tis i méras	to pya-to tees ee-me-ras
bar	To "bar"	To bar
taverna	I tavérna	ee ta-ver-na
café	To kafeneío	to ka-fe-nee-o
fish taverna	I psarotavérna	ee psa-ro-ta-ver-na
grill house	I psistariá	ee psee-sta-rya
wine shop	To oinopoleío	to ee-no-po-lee-o
dairy shop	To galakto-poleío	to ga-lak-to-po-lee-o
restaurant	To estiatório	to e-stee-a-to-ree-o
ouzeri	To ouzerí	to oo-ze-ree
meze shop	To mezedopoleío	To me-ze-do-po-lee-o
take away kebabs	To souvlatzídiko	To soo-vlat-zee-dee-ko
rare	Eláchista psiméno	e-lach-ees-ta psee-me-no
medium	Métria psiméno	met-ree-a psee-me-no
well done	Kalopsiméno	ka-lo-psee-me-no

Basic Food and Drink

English	Greek	Pronunciation
coffee	O Kafés	o ka-fes
with milk	me gála	me ga-la
black coffee	skétos	ske-tos cho-rees
without sugar	chorís záchari	za-cha-ree
medium sweet	métrios	me-tree-os
very sweet	glyk'ys	glee-kees
tea	tsái	tsa-ee
hot chocolate	zestí sokoláta	ze-stee so-ko-la-ta
wine	krasí	kra-see
red	kókkino	ko-kee-no
white	lefkó	lef-ko
rosé	rozé	ro-ze
raki	To rakí	to ra-kee
ouzo	To oúzo	to oo-zo
retsina	I retsína	ee ret-see-na
water	To neró	to ne-ro
octopus	To chtapódi	to chta-po-dee
fish	To psári	to psa-ree
cheese	To tyrí	to tee-ree
halloumi	To chaloúmi	to cha-loo-mee
feta	I féta	ee fe-ta
bread	To psomí	to pso-mee
bean soup	I fasoláda	ee fa-so-la-da
houmous	To houmous	to choo-moos
halva	O chalvás	o chal-vas
meat kebabs	O g'yros	o yee-ros

English	Greek	Pronunciation
Turkish delight	To loukoúmi	to loo-koo-mee
baklava	O mpaklavás	o bak-la-vas
klephtiko	To kléftiko	to klef-tee-ko

Numbers

	Greek	Pronunciation
1	éna	e-na
2	d'yo	thee-o
3	tría	tree-a
4	téssera	te-se-ra
5	pénte	pen-deh
6	éxi	ek-si
7	eptá	ep-ta
8	ochtó	och-to
9	ennéa	e-ne-a
10	déka	the-ka
11	énteka	en-de-ka
12	dódeka	tho-the-ka
13	dekatría	de-ka-tree-a
14	dekatéssera	the-ka-tes-se-ra
15	dekapénte	the-ka-pen-de
16	dekaéxi	the-ka-ek-si
17	dekaeptá	the-ka-ep-ta
18	dekaochtó	the-ka-och-to
19	dekaennéa	the-ka-e-ne-a
20	eíkosi	ee-ko-see
21	eikosiéna	ee-ko-see-e-na
30	triánta	tree-an-da
40	saránta	sa-ran-da
50	penínta	pe-neen-da
60	exínta	ek-seen-da
70	evdomínta	ev-tho-meen-da
80	ogdónta	og-thon-da
90	enenínta	e-ne-neen-da
100	ekató	e-ka-to
200	diakósia	thya-kos-ya
1,000	chília	cheel-ya
2,000	d'yo chiliádes	thee-o cheel-ya-thes
1,000,000	éna ekatomm'yrio	e-na e-ka-to-mee-ree-o
one minute	éna leptó	e-na lep-to
one hour	mía óra	mee-a o-ra
half an hour	misí óra	mee-see o-ra
quarter of an hour	éna tétarto	e-na te-tar-to
half past one	mía kai misí	mee-a keh mee-see
quarter past one	mía kai tétarto	mee-a keh te-tar-to
ten past one	mía kai déka	mee-a keh the-ka
quarter to two	d'yo pará tétarto	thee-o pa-ra te-tar-to
ten to two	d'yo pará déka	thee-o pa-ra the-ka
a day	mía méra	mee-a me-ra
a week	mía evdomáda	mee-a ev-tho-ma-tha
a month	énas mínas	e-nas mee-nas
a year	énas chrónos	e-nas chro-nos
Monday	Deftéra	thef-te-ra
Tuesday	Tríti	tree-tee
Wednesday	Tetárti	te-tar-tee
Thursday	Pémpti	pemp-tee
Friday	Paraskeví	pa-ras-ke-vee
Saturday	Sávvato	sa-va-to
Sunday	Kyriakí	keer-ee-a-kee
January	Ianouários	ee-a-noo-a-ree-os
February	Fevrouários	fev-roo-a-ree-os
March	Mártios	mar-tee-os
April	Aprílios	a-pree-lee-os
May	Máios	ma-ee-os
June	Ioúnios	ee-oo-nee-os
July	Ioúlios	ee-oo-lee-os
August	Avgoustos	av-goo-stos
September	Septémvrios	sep-tem-vree-os
October	Októvrios	ok-to-vree-os
November	Noémvrios	no-em-vree-os
December	Dekémvrios	the-kem-vree-os